Keeping the
FAITH

Keeping the
FAITH

How Applying Spiritual Purpose

to Your Work

Can Lead to Extraordinary Success

ANA MOLLINEDO MIMS

 An *Imprint* of HarperCollins *Publishers*

HarperCollins books may be purchased for educational, business, or
sales promotional use. For information, please write: Special Markets
Department, HarperCollins Publishers, 10 East 53rd Street, New
York, NY 10022.

FIRST EDITION

Designed by Janet M. Evans

Library of Congress Cataloging-in-Publication Data

Mollinedo Mims, Ana.
    Keeping the faith : how applying spiritual purpose to your work
can lead to extraordinary success / Ana Mollinedo Mims.—1st ed.
        p.   cm.
    ISBN: 978-0-06-112592-8
    1. Work—Religious aspects—Christianity. 2. Employees—Religious
life. 3. Success—Religious aspects—Christianity. I. Title.

BT738.5.M65 2007
248.8'8—dc22   2006051715

07 08 09 10 11 ID/RRD 10 9 8 7 6 5 4 3 2 1

There is a God-shaped vacuum
in the heart of every man
which cannot be filled by any created thing,
but only by God the Creator,
made known through Jesus Christ

—BLAISE PASCAL,
mathematician (1623–1662)

Contents

Introduction

I HAD MY FIRST PAYING JOB at the age of fifteen. I worked part time for an insurance company calling people on the phone asking for correct mailing addresses. While I was in high school, I worked as a cashier at a Kmart store. My most recent job has been as a vice president for a Fortune 500 company.

For a number of reasons, the path that my career took was not an expected one for me or others watching the course of my life. I came to the United States from another country as a child. English was not my first language. We—my family and I—had no contacts, no money, not even our own home. As a matter of fact, not too long ago, a longtime girlfriend called me up to let me know she had run into someone who was a colleague of ours when I was twenty-two. My friend shared with this person the various things I had accomplished and places I had lived since those times, and the response she got was "Gee, I never thought she would be that successful."

I am living proof that career success is not just for the lucky or the well connected. Or for those who receive positive reinforcement about their goals in life. It comes from focus, determination, and, most important for me, from a relationship with God. Everything flows from that relationship, including and especially the hours that take up most of our time that we call our work life.

And that's what this book is all about.

*W*HAT DOES CAREER SUCCESS mean to you? How do you or will you measure it? Consider that if you're like most, you are looking at a work life of forty or more years. What is within your power to make those years fulfilling and gratifying?

Maybe you're a student right now, trying to choose an area of study that you hope will lead you toward a good job or career with a good paycheck and lifestyle.

Or you're just starting out in your career and are caught up in all the new challenges you face each day in an entry-level position.

Maybe you work in a service field and you're looking for ways to make more money or work more independently.

Maybe you're midway through a corporate career and you're thinking that it was all kind of a mistake, that you'd be happier if you had made different choices years ago. And should you (could you?) change at this stage of the game?˙

Or maybe you're well established and successful but you're still wondering about the bigger picture in some largely unformed way. You entertain those "Is this all there is?" suspicions.

I believe that the answers or the outcomes in each case will become clearer, and more deeply satisfying, when you are able to shift your line of sight and consider whether what you are doing is what you are supposed to be doing and what it means to blend your working life with a relationship with God. I do believe that, as a result, your definition of success will change as well.

Spiritual values are born from within. They grow and strengthen when we seek to satisfy that "God-shaped vacuum in the heart . . . , which cannot be filled by any created thing, but only by God the Creator." In this day and hour in which we live, more than ever before, a robust, guiding spiritual life is the one element in life we cannot afford to live without.

Today, being employed in America (or anywhere for that matter) is not a comforting state. Job security is largely a thing of the past. Lifelong employment—you're hired, you stay with that company for years, you retire with a decent enough pension—is extremely rare. Pay cuts, outsourcing, downsizing and layoffs, disappearing health benefits—all these things have created fearfulness and uncertainty in a world where we already have enough to worry about.

In this atmosphere, we're all driven to keep up. We're working longer hours than ever before, studies show, and often with smaller staffs and fewer resources. In many jobs, the technology that was supposed to make life easier has actually contributed to making it more stressful. Some of you can remember the days when you left the office and didn't work again until you returned the next morning. Today, cell phones, beepers, faxes, and the BlackBerry device ensure that we are on call and accessible at all hours.

Companies no longer feel great loyalty to their employees, and the feeling is mutual. We've seen that too often the people running the companies cannot be trusted to act with integrity and honesty. In an increasingly global economy, the old walls that added to a sense of job security have crumbled. Someone on another continent might be able to do what you do, just as well and more cheaply. And of course, after the terrorist attacks of September 11, 2001, and continuing warfare, the world feels unsafe, perhaps permanently.

All of this has led so many of us to start questioning our choices: Where do I find security and peace? If I am going to spend so many hours working, am I really where I should be? What's my purpose in life? Who can help me now?

Our spiritual lives and values matter more than ever. We know that instinctively. In a recent Gallup Poll, 70 percent of Americans said they yearned to experience greater personal spiritual growth. We feel a desperate need to look inward and upward and draw strength from something greater than ourselves. That's where the only safe haven is found—in something greater and unmoveable.

As individuals, each one of us is responsible for shaping our destiny. No one will do it for us. Each of us has a calling, a purpose in life. I have discovered that when you reach out to a God who is there, listen to His call, and embark on a journey with Him, then a career path—the one you're meant to be on—opens before you. You might find yourself following some unexpected roads. Or switching gears entirely and heading in another direction. Or doing just what you're doing now, but with greater assurance, deeper satisfaction, and more joy and balance.

There's another aspect to the spirit-led career, and it plays out in the bigger arena. As a culture, we are all richer when the spiritual principles outlined in this book take precedence over the bottom-line mentality that places the highest value on economic success. Our workplaces, wherever they are, should not be colored by greed, dishonesty, lack of loyalty, or cutthroat behavior. This mentality shouldn't be the only one moving forward the world of work. We all need to make a living, support our families, and provide a basic quality of life. I believe that the values outlined in this book, coupled with a relationship with God, will lead any person to success, even if initially adhering to them may be difficult. In the end, you will reap what you sow.

*Y*EARS AGO, I became convinced that I was wired the way I was—that is, I possessed characteristics, personality traits, likes and dislikes, preferences and abilities—for a reason that was tied to my calling and purpose for being on this earth. I believe that each of us is wired in his or her unique way, thanks to a God who is good, who calls, who gives us what we need to accomplish that call, and who assists us in getting there. My conviction fueled a strong desire not to squander the gifts I have or the time I have been given to develop and use them. This, of course, is a journey of a lifetime. Over time, I discovered that standing up to take hold of my purpose required many things, including faith, prayerfulness, humility, integrity, forgiveness, stewardship, and an understanding of what it means to leave behind a legacy.

These are the themes I address in the sections of my book.

The words I have used as chapter titles may sound lofty or abstract or perhaps even somewhat meaningless outside of a religious context. But as you will see, living out the values and imperatives of those faith-based words happens in down-to-earth, concrete ways. It has to do with how you listen, with how and when you ask for help, with expecting appropriate recognition for your talents and commitment, with taking the tough road because it's the right thing, even if no one notices but you or regardless of the outcome. Over my career, I've wrestled with tough choices and thorny problems. More than half a dozen times, I followed job opportunities that required my relocating to a new city where I knew no one. More than once, I coped with exclusionary behavior from bosses and colleagues. I had to make difficult decisions about when and why it was time to move on. And on several occasions I was faced with taking a stand on issues because it was right, ignoring whether it was popular to do so.

The principles I talk about in this book carried me through and served me well. They are the principles that begin with a relationship with God and underlie the spirit-led career. This must be in place in order to receive God's guidance, but the principles don't develop overnight. Almost always, unavoidable consequences come with facing who we are called to be. Failure often precedes success. Success has obligations. And obstacles come in many forms—our own doubts, other people's words and attitudes, family traditions, and more.

As you will see when you read the following chapters, the work experiences I've had and the lessons I've learned from them have come about through my jobs in corporations and in nonprofit organizations. For many years, I have held managerial positions, supervised employees, and been involved in major planning decisions. That's where my talents and my wiring have led me and that's the arena in which these principles have played out. But they are equally valid, critical—and noticeable—wherever your working life takes shape.

For this book, I've talked to a number of people and asked them to tell me their stories. These were men and women, youngish and oldish, working in various fields. Their experiences illuminate the challenges of striving for career success through spiritual values. Their stories show that principles come alive and hold power when you live them, when they are translated from your head to your heart and then to your actions.

I AM EXCITED that you have chosen to read this book and come along with me on a journey that looks at some of the common struggles all people face at various stages of their working lives—remaining true to what you believe, dealing with adversity or prejudice, overcoming obstacles, putting your full energy and attention into what you're doing. From my own experiences, I know that when those difficulties and doubts are confronted in a spiritual way, based on a relationship with God, each can lead to success, growth, and a clearer understanding of yourself, your purpose, and the God who calls us into relationship with Him.

PART ONE

Rebirth

Called to the Journey

I'M AN ORDINARY PERSON. There is nothing particularly special about me compared with countless others. If you came to know me over time, you might notice a few idiosyncrasies.

For example, I hate talking on the phone and I don't like to watch TV. I couldn't tell you who's a pop singer these days or name a top 10 song. Reading is a great pleasure of mine. In terms of style, my clothes, which have to last forever since I don't like to shop, are largely all black and shades of black. I started buying black almost exclusively during my years of traveling on the job, when a day started with a breakfast meeting and ended in a reception at night. I learned to dress in outfits that would look professional from early morning and into the evening. But the truth is

I've loved black since I was a kid. I read once that black is defined as the presence of all color, so on that basis, I have always considered myself very colorful.

I can't cook, though I love to entertain. My friends call me the Hispanic Martha Stewart. I've developed a repertoire of interesting, delicious vegetarian appetizers that I like to serve, all neatly set out on pretty plates with little printed cards next to the dishes, so people know what they're eating. I enjoy the art of display.

In my next career, in fact, I might choose to be an interior decorator. Mixing fabrics and colors and pulling it all together in a way that feels peaceful and warm and unique is deeply satisfying to me. Again, I like the art of display. I believe home should be an expression of who you are. I'm big on having personal pictures around my house, telling a history of where I've been and about my family and my friends.

So again, a few idiosyncrasies, but nothing special. I'm an ordinary person living an ordinary life.

However, one night, years ago, I had an extraordinary experience that changed my life and subsequently who I have become and set me on a spiritual journey that shaped my decisions from an early age. This experience brought me to a place where I have grown to hold certain things true:

- I believe in destiny.

- I believe each of us has a path that points toward that destiny.

- I believe in God, the Lord God. Not Allah, not a univeral power, not an energy, but in the Living God who became man through the person of Jesus Christ.

- I believe that I am here for a purpose, not because of some random occurrence or decision by my parents.

- I believe events in my life happen for a reason, not by accident.

- I believe that we have free will, and when we cede that free will to God's purpose and plan, in life and in business, we will find ourselves on a journey that will fulfill and elate us, by no one's standards but His own.

I want to tell you about that night—what led up to it and where it led me.

I WAS AN EIGHTEEN-YEAR-OLD cuban-born girl, living in South Florida with my siblings and immigrant parents. I was basically a good girl—advanced student in school, not doing drugs or drinking, not playing around with boys. I was busy with part-time jobs and schoolwork. But during the previous year, at the age of seventeen, I had started feeling as if everything was in shambles. Personally, I felt I was a mess.

I was struggling with decisions about what to study and what to do with my life. And struggling with the family dynamics that most teenagers struggle with did not help either. I seemed to be growing and changing faster and to a greater degree than my parents could keep up with, and of course that was causing conflicts. The conflicts usually centered around typical and unsurprising issues: I was the oldest child, and so paving the way in new areas—determining my own schedule, getting my own car, and so on. But many of my internal struggles related to how I wanted to worship. The old rules, so many of them learned through our traditional church, weren't working or making much sense for me anymore. I remember wondering *What is happening? Where is this all heading?* It was a terrible discomfort clouding my thoughts and consuming my days. I suppose my unspoken, still unformed plea was *God, where are you? I need answers and I need help.*

On the particular night that I'm describing, it was a year later, at age eighteen, and I was sitting in my room. I'd finished studying, everyone else was asleep, and the house was quiet. I began praying the Our Father, my common practice. Suddenly I sat up and thought, *This does not mean anything to me, this rote, repetitive prayer that I was taught and that I've almost mindlessly prayed all my life.*

Looking up at the ceiling, I thought I'd try what I believed was impossible (at least back then)—talking directly to God. I'd never attempted that before. I said:

God, I know you're there. Inside, I know you have to be there. But I need some help. I have questions that I can't answer and nobody else seems to be able to answer for me. I want you to talk with me the way you did with Abraham and Moses. I want to have a relationship with you and talk to you directly. I don't want to go through all these other steps and all this other stuff to have a relationship with you. I don't know if I'm saying something wrong here, but I can't pray the old way any longer. It doesn't mean anything to me and it doesn't have any connection to the circumstances I am in. I'm going through motions, meaningless motions.

I remember saying those words.

In the midst of this one-way conversation, some words from my childhood Sunday school teacher popped into my mind. I'd sought her out a year earlier and spoken to her about my misgivings and my concerns about religion and my faith. She told me then that it was about surrendering. It's about accepting that God did, in fact, become like me and died for me, and that He has a plan for me as a result, a plan that's personal and unique.

When I thought of my teacher's comments, I said: *God, if what I need to do to find peace and to get these questions answered is to give you my life and not try to figure out how it's all going to work out on my own, then here it is. Here's my life. Come take control. Come walk with me, come talk to me, come show me why I'm here, why I'm wired the way I'm wired. Show me the meaning of some of this stuff that overwhelms me. Just come and be in my life, and I'll follow. You can see tomorrow; I cannot. So you can tell me what decision I need to make today to have a better tomorrow.*

Then I went to sleep.

I woke up the next morning, and I have to say, it was pretty weird. Nothing outwardly dramatic had happened to me. No mystical visitation. I didn't even remember all that had happened the night before, just falling asleep somewhat exhausted and drained. When I woke up, the picture was the same. It was Saturday. My mother was expecting my sister and me to get up and to help her clean the house, the way we did every weekend.

But there was an overwhelming sense, almost a presence in the center of my chest, that something was different. Something that I had prayed the night before had altered my sight, though I didn't know yet exactly what or how. It felt, almost, as if someone had dropped information inside my brain, information I still needed to sort out.

My circumstances hadn't changed. And yet I knew I was profoundly changed.

First Steps on a Transforming Journey

We expect God to fix our circumstances, make them different. That the person who's giving us trouble will become benign. That the school, the job, the house we don't like will be replaced by something better and brighter. I quickly learned that these changes are usually not part of the rebirth. In fact, God is interested in whatever it is in our heart that's blocking us from being able to be effective in those very situations. So many times, people miss the experience of God because of an expectation that God will come in a certain way to accomplish a certain outcome they desire. But God is God. He arrives on His terms. This doesn't mean He won't ultimately change the circumstances. But while we are looking at the endgame, He's looking at the journey that will lead us there, because it's in the journey that we are transformed.

For me, as an eighteen-year-old, my first step was an understanding that I could not return to our family church. Something so significant had happened within me that I was aware that our church was no longer the place for me. And believe me, given how I was raised, that conclusion was not inevitable or a logical next step. But I knew I just could not, in good conscience, worship in the old manner again, though I had nothing substantial in the way of proof. I simply understood that God had visited me in a personal way, as evidenced by the peace and the sense of joy I felt, which surpassed anything I could explain.

The particulars were still foggy. As I was going about my Saturday routines, I thought, *What do I do now? Where am I going to go? What does all this mean?*

I wound up calling my childhood Sunday school teacher, whom I hadn't spoken to in a year but whose advice back then had initiated so much. I told her that the wildest thing had just happened, and I shared my experience. She listened with care; when I was done, she invited me to visit church with her the next Sunday. To my astonishment, she said she was now attending a nondenominational church, and she added, "You know what? You ultimately have to feel comfortable with whatever setting God is going to put you in. And that means you're going to have to try some different places, and hear for yourself His voice, about where you should be."

That's what I started doing shortly thereafter. And ever since that time, in the various cities and places I've lived, I have always found where I should be, sometimes through trial and error, and always with prayer. I've found my church, my spiritual home and community.

Hearing His Voice

And now, let me backtrack again and fill in some history leading up to my first real conversation with God.

Being eighteen suggests a lot. That's a major time of transition for most kids, after all: reaching the end of the high school years, making decisions about college or jobs coming up, splitting away from the family more and more, and establishing independence as a full-fledged adult, or one who's at least partly there.

I experienced some of all that. However, I don't put a lot of stock in the fact that I was in my teens when I was called into relationship with God. That is, I would not describe or explain my extraordinary experience in terms of teenage angst. I've never marked passages in age segments. I am still today not someone who has angst at the thought of turning thirty or forty. Age has never affected me greatly. My dad always said that you are as old as you think you are, and whatever your life is about in the moment has to do with what you feel inside. I have always shared his attitude.

But my deep, personal experience of God at that time, the experience that really became the lens through which I began to view everything else, did not come entirely out of the blue. It was a cumulative process that I believe started with a desire just really to know who God is and not to have that filtered through or interpreted by other people.

Mine was a traditional Hispanic family. Life at home was fairly strict and regimented. We were raised with the understanding, for example, that a girl didn't call someone a boyfriend lightly. We did not go out alone with boys but had social evenings either with groups of friends or with one or the other of our parents. There was a good amount of parental supervision. That was part of our culture. That was the deal.

As early as I can remember, God played a central role in our lives. As a result we embraced the sense of always being thankful and the necessity of worship. From the time I was a young girl, my mother taught me: "When you wake up in the morning, Ana, before your feet even touch the floor, thank God for a new day. Your first thought upon becoming conscious should be toward God and thanksgiving." This was one of her great gifts to me, and I still practice her advice to this day. And I can tell you that when a day starts out moving too fast, when my mind is overloaded with thoughts of all I have to get done and I don't give thanks to God before my feet hit the ground and only remember when I'm brushing my teeth, there's a twitch inside me. A feeling: *Oh, how could I have gone this far, to get to the bathroom sink and brush my teeth and not yet have given thanks for a new day?*

Then there was the church. The church was central to our family life, and that was another part of the deal. You will go to church on Sunday, no questions asked. You will take the sacraments, no questions asked. Confirmation, communion, all of that was expected. And family came first, even if that meant above God, something I no longer hold to be true today at that level, but there it was.

I had followed the rules. I had taught Sunday school in my early teens. And then I began to question. I could not understand why God spoke to all those people in the Bible but didn't speak to us anymore. At least that was the doctrinal background: God does not speak directly to people; he speaks through others in spiritual authority. Increasingly, I'd started to think, *Okay, what's that all about?* I also didn't get all the doctrinal practices.

I do believe that many people entertain questions along these lines and that they seek answers through other people, not in a one-on-one with God. My religious background, too, was all about allowing others to couch and position and format God for me. More and more, that didn't interest me. I began mentioning to clergy and people in authority in my church the questions I was mulling over in my mind, and they didn't have answers either—at least not the definitive answers I was looking for. Their answers were the ones we had always been given: "God works in mysterious ways" and "Who can know the thoughts of God?" and "That is what our doctrine teaches us." That wasn't enough anymore, and somehow I knew there was more.

But my Sunday school teacher, a woman who'd known me since I was about six years old, began sharing something quite different with me, to my surprise. She said, "Well, Ana, some of the questions you have are those that the Holy Spirit is prompting in you. He wants you to begin a journey in order to seek and to find Him. It's really about surrendering your life and accepting who Christ is supposed to be in your life."

I was seventeen. And that wasn't making a lot of sense to me. But she and I had a couple of such talks. Clearly her insights and suggestions must have lodged somewhere in my mind, because a year later, I had my conversation with God on the night that changed me forever.

He Comes When You're Ready to Hear

Looking back, I believe my Sunday school teacher was right. God had to have been prompting me, pushing me forward, through the questions and dissatisfactions I struggled with.

For many people, reaching for a relationship with God might come much later, one aspect of the famous midlife crisis: *I've been out in the world, had my career, made my money, bought the vacation house, and now? Is there something more? Is this to be the full expression of my one life?* Then starts the search for a deeper meaning, and perhaps this search ends in peace and a sense of purpose. Maybe it doesn't. At the other end, a teenager just into the years when Mom and Dad can no longer dictate all her comings and goings or impose their beliefs might begin to question those dictates, and frequently the result is to reject the whole package: *My parents made me go to church all these years, and the church all these years has told me what to believe and how to think, and you know what? I've decided it's all*

hogwash. There can be a turning away from anything having to do with religion and the life of the Spirit.

I am convinced from my experiences over the years
that many people deeply desire a relationship with God,
but perhaps not in the way that dogma teaches it or tells us
it must come about. God can call you at any time. As I began
discovering the Bible, I found a lot to think about. There
were many moments of *Aha, okay, I'm beginning to get it.*
And God, you must have something significant in mind for me,
not significant in the way humans define it, but in a bigger
sense. And as for age, Abraham was in his seventies. David
was anointed king of Israel at age thirteen, fifteen years
before he actually took the position. In one section of the
New Testament, Paul writes to Timothy, whom he is mentoring, telling his young acolyte not to let people despise
his age.

God will speak to each of us in the manner in which
and at the time each of us can hear. These messages move
our hearts and souls in ways that will move nobody else.
I do believe that God and people interact every single
day. It's up to us whether we hear. One of the truths I've
learned about God is that He's a consummate gentleman.
He will never force Himself on you. I think He takes even
more seriously than we do the fact that He created us with
free will.

At the Heart of Relationship

People might say I had a mystical experience on that night I talked to God. I don't see it that way. Maybe at the time I might have called it supernatural, if pressed and for want of a better word. Today, I know that connecting with God is a totally down-to-earth, naturally supernatural thing. It is in no way weird or crazy or out of this world; it brings uncommon common sense in a practical manner to life and to the decisions we make, day in and day out.

In fact, the more I walk the path, the more it's like dealing with and living with another person, a human being right here and now. And that's why I talk about *relationship*, a term that feels to me more accurate and more to the essence of the matter even than *belief*.

My relationship with my husband, the person closest to me, mirrors much of what I've come to build in my relationship with God. Marrying my life to another person, I gave him control, he gave me control, and we began the process of becoming one. Obviously, there are differences. You do not say to your spouse, "You're in complete control of me." You do say—if you are shaping a Christian marriage—"I am choosing to be one with you. I take on all of your stuff and you take on all of mine, and we're no longer two separate people. Though we may have individual callings, those callings are now intertwined."

God is not going to come to me and tell me I'm called to

be on a mission in Africa while my husband comes to me and says, "Maybe, but God's telling me I'm supposed to be in corporate life here in New York City." God is not going to speak to us that way anymore. That means when our callings seem divergent, one or the other or each of us has to go back and get clear with God—through prayer and prayerful thought, through asking the questions, exploring the options, and listening for His guidance.

You don't enter a marriage thinking you're going to do it on your own terms—at least not if you want a union that lasts a lifetime. There's a lot of compromise. At the same time, there are actions and behaviors that are not up for discussion, that are nonnegotiable. Having an affair? That's a nonnegotiable. It will not be part of the marriage. It's the same with God: *Thou shalt have no other gods before me.* What are "other gods"? Anything that commands your attention or affection more than He does, including work or hobbies.

I'm not married just in certain places or at certain times, and I don't just consult my husband on some issues here and there. I'm married all day long, everywhere I go, whether others I meet are aware of that fact or not. I talk over with my spouse all the decisions that affect my life, because I have chosen to be one with him out of love.

Over twenty years, my relationship with God has grown in the same way. He's the person I first speak to when I have a decision to make. My confidant. Do I have regular prayer times and devotion times? I do. But more than that, the conversation is an ongoing, all-day-long, everyday dialogue, really no different from one with any other person with whom I'm deeply involved like my husband.

I reached the point of understanding that having the kind of relationship God wants to have with me, with each of us, is the equivalent of being married in a spiritual way. And that understanding blew away any notion that He lays down rules and regulations and that if I break the rules, He'll be angry with me. No, His concern originates from a place of love. When I more and more began to feel God's love, I realized how merciful and full of grace He has been toward me. There is a song we sing in church called "Grace, God's Unmerited Favor." There's nothing you do to earn it; it comes from love. God says, *I'm giving you this, just because.*

When we start looking at the connection in a more relational way and in a less religious/dogmatic way, then we see God for who He really is, not how we've come to know Him through our doctrines.

Breaking Down the Walls

With my friends or acquaintances, I never talk about church, unless someone asks me specifically what church I attend. It's not about that.

I bump into many people who call themselves Christian, and as I come to know them, as I observe how they handle themselves in business situations and elsewhere, I see the difference between labeling oneself a Christian and having a true relationship with God. For many, their religious identity comes with family tradition: My mother was Lutheran, my grandparents were Lutheran, I'm Lutheran. My father was a Pentecostal preacher; I'm not a preacher myself—I'm a retailing executive—but I go to the Pentecostal church. The real question is this: Does belonging to a particular religious tradition or going to a particular church bring you into relationship with God? And the questions that follow are these: Does that relationship carry over into everything else? Do you bring it into your working life, into the office, into the way you go about earning your living?

Many do carry that relationship everywhere. I would say that many more do not. You can read the Bible and attend church services, but it means little without a relationship with God and the willingness to be governed by it— the willingness to surrender and be committed to His guidance in how you conduct all your daily affairs. We don't like those words, *surrender* and *commitment*. But they speak to having the courage of our convictions.

It's easy to compartmentalize: *Here's where I go on Sunday; here's what I believe on Sunday. And then this is what I do the rest of the week.* Or maybe: *This is who I am at home, and that's who I am at work.* What I'm saying in this book is that in order to live a truly Spirit-led life and maintain a truly Spirit-led career, you have to bring down the walls of those compartments. You cannot be of one mind and nature here and another there. The Bible calls that being "double-minded." I cannot claim to be a person who believes in God and then remove that construct from the rest of my life whenever it is easier or more convenient for me to do so.

I believe that a good and true relationship with God tells me how to live a good and true life and that life can happen anywhere—in any venue, any arena, any office building or workplace. Because I am one with God doesn't mean I necessarily feel a call to be out in the mission field. The mission field is everywhere I go. Some people are clearly called to work for their faith, to be missionaries or to be in some similar way involved in activities with a spiritual intent. But it's not necessary in order to serve God. Look in the Bible and you will see that many of those individuals were called to be heads of government, business people, tradespeople, judges. It wasn't until later that a select few were called to be the disciples and missionaries. God did not sequester Himself; He became a man and one of us in the person of Christ. He stripped himself of everything godly and put Himself into one of our shells and dwelt among us.

You may not be entirely comfortable with this "God

talk." You may even say that you don't believe in God. But consider this: You have an instinct deep within about right and wrong, good and bad. If you hold a conversation with a colleague or friend that's difficult and uncomfortable, but the right and needed thing to do, you feel both relieved and uplifted in some way. If you act poorly, if you do something dishonest or with malicious intent, there's a little undercurrent in the back of your mind that unsettles you. Maybe you put effort into trying to justify your behaviors to yourself.

You might call that conscience or character or strength of will or a well-developed sense of morality. To me, it's the instinct toward God; it's the God-shaped vacuum in your heart calling you into a relationship with Him. It is the inherent knowledge within the soul that there is God.

That relationship, that instinct, prompts us to respond to all that comes at us in our working lives. It is borne out in the principles I talk about in the following chapters: facing obstacles or uncertainties with faith and courage, behaving with integrity, demonstrating appropriate humility, forgiving those who should be forgiven, having a sense of stewardship and service, and leaving a worthwhile legacy.

Making the Connection

So let's look at the mission field of daily life, the nitty-gritty, the getting up in the morning and going to work. Maybe, in the context of this chapter, I can call it moving from the sacred to the profane. Here are several career-related scenarios, from my own experiences and those of other people who have shared their stories with me for this book. Some of the stories I talk about further in the following chapters.

Right now, a few random snapshots:

Earlier in my career, I was often asked to take on assignments involving contacts with Hispanic clients or interests. That made sense, because I speak Spanish fluently and because I had useful business knowledge about the community. At the same time, those assignments were added on to my regular job requirements and focus. The result was fifteen-hour workdays and many frustrations.

Sally, a clerical worker and single mother in her mid-twenties, was living "a very hand-to-mouth existence," she said. One month when she faced an unexpected but critical expense, she asked her officemate and friend for a small loan until their next payday. The officemate advanced her the money, tacking on interest and having Sally sign an IOU. Sally was deeply embarrassed and couldn't see how she and the officemate could remain friends.

As a supervisor in the ad department of a pharmaceutical company, Max managed three employees. He became aware that one of them was making end runs around him, going to Max's boss with progress reports on their work and requests for feedback. Max's inclination was to fire this young man, though in most ways he was a good worker.

Calling herself a private person and one who hates office politics, Sheila had a deep aversion to the schmoozing, as she called it, that seemed to go along with her job. Her company orchestrated a number of events that were combined business–social affairs; she was expected to show up and be seen circulating. Sheila felt like a phony, making conversation with people who didn't particularly interest her.

Cara was asked to give a talk before the marketing meeting–think tank session that was held annually by her magazine. She'd never done that before and was uncertain about how to present a performance review and future plans for her department, especially since a new editor in chief had recently come on board. Cara tried for two weeks to get a meeting with the new editor, but the woman never answered her requests. Cara began to get an uncomfortable feeling that she was being set up to flop.

Joe worked for a corporation that had in place flextime and telecommuting policies, ostensibly offering valued employees the opportunity to self-manage aspects of their jobs. Joe took advantage of that opportunity for a six-month stretch, working from home two days a week. At his year-end review, he was passed over for an expected bonus, and he wondered if he was being singled out because he'd often been away from the office.

Does that all sound far removed from the ideas I've talked about earlier, the conversation with God and the search for His guidance? It's not. Is there a Spirit-led way to think about or to take action in each of those rough patches or dilemmas or tricky situations? Can you make the connection? I say, yes, absolutely.

The way to illuminate the principles is to live them. What happens when tough times pop up? How do I deal with business issues? Why have I made the decisions I've made, and how have I made them? What have I been willing to do and what have I not been willing to do? What motivates me in one direction or another?

O VER THE YEARS, I have seen that my life is indeed a journey and that my faith and trust in God's purpose for me is a dynamic force in my decisions and actions on a daily basis. In the following chapters, I want to show you how that works. I call these sections principles. They might be called rules for the journey or lessons learned along the path. They capture my experiences as a woman, as a member of an ethnic minority, and as a Christian—for the combination of these three aspects of me have shaped my life story and, in particular, my career.

PART TWO

Principles of the
Spirit-Led Career

ONE

Faith

The Substance of Things Not Seen,

the Evidence of Things Hoped For

FAITH COMES FIRST. It is trust in God and in His purpose for me. It's believing that behind each door that opens, one after the other, is what should be. Each folds into and promotes my mission in this life. Faith is assurance and conviction that the things not seen will be all right and the things hoped for will come about if they are part of the plan for me.

Faith leads to courage. To facing adversity. To overcoming obstacles, from without and from within. And to meeting opportunity with conviction and drive.

I think that in the world of work, faith challenges play out in one of two ways. For many people, faith comes into the picture when there's a change to make. That might be an unavoidable change imposed from the outside world, or a quiet and growing conviction within that another, better, truer working life can be found. Do I take a step forward, switch jobs, maybe go out on a limb and try something completely new, even though I don't know a whole lot about what I'm heading into? Can I trust the voice inside that's telling me that this is my purpose? And then for some people, it's the reverse. Do I hang in and hang on to what I'm doing because I believe it's right? Even though I'm being battered and tested and the naysayers are all around?

For me, my whole career path seems to have been a matter of stepping out on faith, with absolute trust but insufficient information. Each opening door didn't seem entirely logical or one I would have predicted. Some took me to places that were strange and new and not at all comfortable. There were times I had no idea how I'd be able to accomplish what I was hired to do.

Faith is what kept me stepping forward anyway.

Here's one of my favorite ways to explain the essence of faith: You know that you know that you know. In choosing to take each of those steps, I knew what I knew what I knew. That sureness had two roots. Above all, there was my surrender to God's will, the rebirth I described in an earlier chapter. He was leading me, and I knew it. And then there was the example my parents set for me. My earliest lessons in stepping out on faith came from my parents' examples and words. Those lessons still resonate inside me.

I want to share with you some of my parents' story, and mine as a child and young adult. The details of our stories show what a faith-based road map can look like.

Move from the Known to the Unknown

In 1967, we boarded what was to be one of the last of the freedom flights from Havana, Cuba, to Miami. I was two years old.

What I remember most from the two years I lived in Cuba was the sense of fear in the air. Even young children will pick up on emotions, although they don't quite understand what's going on, and I knew something was very, very wrong. My face in the old pictures is solemn and serious. It's not a smiling, happy face, not a little girl's face.

In particular, I remember the airport on the day we left. I remember being searched and seeing guns and men in military uniforms. On the plane, people were crying. The trip from Cuba to Florida is only ninety miles, so we took a forty-five-minute plane ride, or perhaps it was a little longer with the older engines back then. But I remember it being seemingly endless—dreadful, tense, sad, especially because of the people crying. Something about that brief experience imprinted itself in my mind, and that imprint is still very real today. Much later, I realized that those people knew they weren't going back. They were leaving home for good.

Our small group consisted of my parents, me, my four-week-old sister, and my grandmother in her seventies, my mother's mother. Between us, we carried only four small suitcases. The suitcases had been looked through at the airport. Any items that were considered valuable and worth keeping had been taken away from us. My father had a Patek Philippe watch; they removed it from his wrist. They removed wedding bands. Amazingly, my mother was able to sneak out a pair of tiny diamond stud earrings, suitable for a young child. In our culture, babies receive a significant gift at birth, one to carry with them throughout their lives. The earrings were my gift when I was born and have now been passed on to my daughter.

So that was how we left, on a Pan Am jet, granted political asylum, with literally nothing but what we were wearing and four bags. After ours, there were maybe two more freedom flights out, and then the United States severed all ties with Cuba.

My parents have now spent more years in the United States than they did in the old country. But what it took for them in the way of faith and courage to walk forward, I could fully appreciate only as I grew and learned.

Just imagine this: There's a knock on your door. A government agent enters and announces that you no longer own anything; the government now owns your home and belongings. In addition, unless you adopt their cause and beliefs, you will not be able to find a job anywhere. You're now broke.

That's the way it was for us and many others around the world.

In Cuba, my father and his family had land and raised cattle. My mother and her family had always lived in the city. They met, my mom and dad, on a blind date, married within the same year, and applied for political asylum during the time my mother was pregnant with me. As it turned out, the process took so long and our exit was so delayed that my sister was also born in Cuba, two years later. We lived in Havana, but my family's lands and its income were confiscated sometime after the revolution.

Years later, when I was in college, I asked my parents how they had arrived at the decision to leave their country. What were their thoughts and feelings, and what was it like? My father said this: "We looked around, and we realized there was no future there. We didn't believe in what the government stood for, and things were going to become only increasingly more difficult, and now we had a child on the way. Was that the kind of environment we wanted our child to grow up in? What kind of life would the child have in that place? We understood there would be risks in applying to leave. We knew that. But the staying would have been for a lifetime."

Yet it was also so painful for them to go. Two of my

uncles had preceded us to the United States. The remainder of a very large tribe would stay behind. Standing for what is right is often not easy in the short term.

There was a tradition in my dad's family: Every Sunday the family gathered at my grandparents' house for dinner. We still carry on that tradition with my parents. I don't live near them now, but my brother and sister still attend Sunday dinner at my parents' house. Before we left Cuba, my parents went to Sunday dinner as usual. My father told me the story of that night. We were leaving the next day. The flight was arranged; the time had at last arrived. But my dad did not—could not—tell his parents he was leaving the country, because he knew it would simply break their hearts. As we left, my grandfather said, "We'll see you next week, then," and my father replied, "Yes, next week at dinner."

He never saw them alive again. He returned to Cuba for both their funerals, and I think those were the only times I've seen him cry.

Start Anew

So we found ourselves in a totally different country with a totally different culture. We began rebuilding our lives.

In the late 1960s, being Hispanic was not as hip as it perhaps is today. There was no Ricky Martin or Jennifer

Lopez. No Telemundo or *Sábado Gigante*. Gloria Estefan was singing only in Spanish.

Miami was not what it is today. When Cubans first began arriving, the city was not ready for what was about to happen to it. It was not the welcoming melting pot for people from Latin American countries that it is now, but instead very much the quintessential 1960s deep South. We stuck out like sore thumbs, and people let us know it in various unpleasant ways.

We went to live with my uncle, my mother's brother, and his wife and family. It was a crowded household, ten people sharing a two-bedroom apartment. My dad found a job driving trucks for a meatpacking company. At night, he washed dishes at a pizza place down the street.

Our lives really centered on what was needed in order to eat, keep a roof over our heads, and make sure the kids— me, my sister, and eventually my brother—got to school and got an education. When I did start school, I knew very little English, and there were perhaps only three or four other Hispanic students besides me. We attended a public school; we couldn't afford to attend a private or parochial school, which was my parents' preference. We were on the government lunch program, and often there were separate areas for the children receiving assistance, lining up displaying our little cards that marked us as among the poor.

My grandmother lived with us until she died. Not having known my father's parents, I felt that her presence added to the feeling of family history. It was a household run very much by the adults, not the children. That was typical of the time in general, but there was a strong cultural element for us as well. We were not allowed to go in our rooms and shut the door if a school friend came over for an afternoon or evening, for example. Friends were considered to be visiting everyone in the house; whatever anybody had to say, it could and should be said before all of us.

For me, it was like growing up in a schizophrenic world—trying to learn a new culture, a new language, yet still living by the morals and rules of the old country we had come from. Today I'm grateful for the schizophrenia, the split between accepting old-world attitudes and adapting to new-world events and expectations. I'm thankful because I read, write, and speak English and Spanish with equal facility. I have an understanding of my culture and where I came from that helps me define where I'm headed and gives me a life perspective that I would not otherwise have. But when you're a child and then a young teenager in those circumstances, it's tough.

If it was tough or confusing for me, it was surely more so for my parents. What they remembered was a conservative life on an island in the 1940s and 1950s. Life in the United States in the late 1960s and the 1970s could only seem to them totally radical and crazy and occasionally shocking.

I sometimes wondered if they longed for the old Cuba. And I'm not entirely sure of the answer. But one of their great strengths, one of the demonstrations of their faith, was the ability to focus on immediate circumstances. That was their lesson to their children: *Look at what's directly in front of you; that doesn't mean you don't see the forest for the trees, but in times of crisis or difficult transitions, the trees must get your full attention. Don't allow yourself to be overwhelmed by the immensity of the obstacles, don't dillydally, don't become paralyzed. Take action.*

For them the thought was *All right, we're in a new country; we are not starting a life here entertaining the dream that we're going back. This is home now.* They used to tell us, "We're not returning to Cuba; we must learn how to survive and thrive in this culture."

Overcome Discouragement, from Without and Within

When I started college at sixteen, my aim was to become a pediatrician. I thought I would help people, give of myself to children. Then, at age eighteen, I had the experience in which God became intensely real and intensely personal to me, and it left me profoundly changed. I asked the questions *Why am I here? Why am I wired the way I'm wired?*

What is my purpose? And later: *Am I really meant to become a doctor?* As I asked, I began to realize that the answers I thought I had were no longer the answers I was hearing. One major outcome of that growing realization was to abandon my plans to be a pediatrician and to switch my major from premed to political science.

I wasn't entirely sure why. I understood that there would be a lot of reading involved, a lot of research, and a line of study that was new to me. Equally important were the thoughts *How will I make a living? What on earth can I do with a degree in political science? Who even knows what that is exactly?*

My parents, for their part, were extremely skeptical and not at all excited. A degree in political science—unlike a medical degree, for example—did not necessarily lead to a career at which I could make a living. And this was no small decision, on all our parts. My parents had no money to pay for college. I got only partial scholarships. There were not many scholarships and grants then for women or minorities, or even easily accessed information about what was available. No hopping on the Internet to discover my options, if I had any. Diversity wasn't even talked about; interest groups and organizations for minorities were not as prevalent or powerful or well funded, if they existed at all as they are today. So for me it was limited financial aid, supplemented with a mix of part-time jobs as I could find them.

Political science classes were heavily male dominated, with a high level of competition, and my gender, coupled with my cultural background, made my path even rockier. If I had not learned from childhood sports that being a girl was not popular in some arenas, college reminded me. There were almost no other female students in my area. Neither were there female professors I could look to for encouragement and as examples in this line of study.

In addition, the messages around me were hardly encouraging. People I talked to—my pastor, friends, and even some professors—suggested that I probably would go into teaching eventually and should use my degree that way. Or possibly, I would become an attorney, which was a popular career at the time. And becoming an attorney was something my family could more easily understand.

None of this resonated with me for reasons I had not yet understood.

Yet I remained calm and assured. How can I describe it? Not an emotion so much or a thought, but rather a sense, a knowing: *I'm in the center of what I'm supposed to be doing right now. I don't understand where it's heading, but it's right, because I'm at peace about it. This is the right road.*

Throughout the rest of my college days, later in graduate school, and still later as I moved through my career, again and again I experienced the sense of knowing and peace with each step forward and as each door opened. Because He has been faithful every step of the way, I have faith that God's presence will guide anyone willing to seek Him, at any age or life stage. That's one of the great things about God. Bend your knee and incline your ear, and He will speak to you, regardless of what you have or don't have, regardless of how old you are, regardless of where you come from or what you have done. All He needs is a willing heart and a listening ear. I was willing to turn to Him with a life question that I knew only He could answer, and He did. The answer was not *Do this here because you're going there.* I simply experienced a still voice inside that assured me, *This is the way. Walk in it*, and I followed it.

The voices outside were another matter. Often, in school and in the community in which I lived, those voices told me that a Hispanic, and perhaps especially a Hispanic woman, could go only so far in terms of career advancement. There was no expectation at that time, for women or minorities, that taking a bold and different route to success was an option. And I certainly did not see many Hispanic women in leadership positions to give me the impression that I could make it as well. Remember the woman my friend ran into in the last chapter who never thought I would be successful? She was one of those voices.

Despite their reservations about my prospects, their puzzlement over my choice of study and where it might lead, my parents were emotionally supportive, especially my father. He said to me: "Don't listen to the things people tell you. They are speaking out of ignorance and fear. Focus on your studies. Someday it will all pay off. Don't let anyone convince you there is something you cannot do because you are a woman. Don't listen to people who think like that. Forgive them, and don't become like them. Someday people aren't going to care if you are a man or a woman or where you come from. They are only going to care if you can get the job done."

I valued his confidence and his conviction; his words still ring true.

Still, I wrestled with many changes, even within the family and to a greater degree than before. For some time, I had felt a little like the black sheep of the family. Still, I felt I was different from my brother and sister. I knew that I thought differently from my parents in many respects. Was that because I was the oldest sibling? Or was it because I was raised in the schizophrenia of Cuban and American cultures? My life's purpose seemed to be leading me out into another world. What exactly was the difference in me? What was it that was driving me that did not seem to be driving my siblings or some others around me?

Here I was halfway through college, still living at home, making decisions that no one really understood, and sometimes that included me. I no longer wanted to be a doctor, and I was studying this other thing that was largely a mystery, with no clear-cut direction toward a stable career. I was no longer in my family's church but was attending and becoming active in a very different kind of church. My God was even different. I went from feeling that I slightly stuck out at home to definitely sticking out at home!

The push and pull of sometimes seemingly conflicting entities—my parents' confidence and my parents' fears— all would even out over time. And I learned so much in those years about adversity and overcoming obstacles. I learned that adversity sometimes involves breaking out of a family mold or family expectations. It may be what you face within yourself: *Can I really do this? What are other people saying about what I can and can't do, and should I listen to them?* Once you're on the path that you sense is right, then it's adversity from within that environment, as I discovered again and again. But adversity can lead to growth, if you choose to let it—growth not just for you but also for your family and those around you, as I later discovered.

We cannot be deeply moved and changed without upheaval and disturbance somewhere. It just doesn't happen. It's the social theory of thesis and antithesis, chaos before order.

See the Vision, If Only Its Dim Outlines

As I finished, I had a mental picture of what I wanted to be doing ten years later. I consciously and in a disciplined way thought: *What are the steps? Let me work backward. If I want to be at place XYZ ten years from now, because that's what I'm feeling within, then what experiences should I go after in order to be able to stand and walk in those shoes?*

What was the vision? It was about a certain role I would be fulfilling. It had nothing to do with money or where I'd be living. It was more about the use of my talents, what I've been calling here my wiring. I am wired the way I am for a reason, as each of us is. Focus on your talents, and that focus enables you to realize that you are specially created for a unique purpose.

And what I saw ten years down the road was me working in a business setting, using a passion and talents I believed I had communicating and formulating messages, representing issues, and interacting with people. Looking ten years beyond that, I pictured myself running a non-profit organization. *Advocacy* isn't quite the word for it, but something along those lines. The vision was still fuzzy. I hadn't had a real job yet. I'd been a cashier, secretary, receptionist, aerobics teacher, the things you do to work your way through school.

As it turned out, my first job was not in corporate life but in government, in Washington, D.C. Shortly before I graduated, the president of my college mentioned an opportunity in a Florida congressman's office. I applied, I was accepted, and I made the move. At age twenty, still sleeping in the little twin bed of my childhood, I packed a few things in boxes and shipped them ahead of me. I'd never been away from home, never been out of Florida, didn't know a soul in Washington. My dad was nervous. My mom was bordering on hysterical about my leaving home.

On the job, I was on the bottom rung and meagerly compensated. Going to the occasional official reception as a representative of our office was wonderful, because at least I'd get to eat something more than my soup and crackers back at the apartment I shared with four roommates. I didn't enjoy the hardship, but I loved the adventure. In D.C., too, I rarely had contact with Hispanic people, whereas in South Florida, of course, I was mostly with my parents, their friends, my family, a culture I knew. So this was educational, to observe how being Hispanic was perceived when there weren't many of us around.

Here's what followed over, roughly, the next fifteen years:

- A move back to Miami, working in the congressman's office there, and a return to school for a graduate degree
- Lobbying and legislative work for the credit union trade association and the retailers' trade association in Florida, jobs that took me to Tallahassee

· A move into the corporate arena, with
responsibility for government relations and
public affairs for large companies in the
pharmaceutical field, and relocations to Bir-
mingham, Alabama, and Atlanta, Georgia

· The role of executive director of the Martin
Luther King Center in Atlanta, which was
then followed by executive positions as vice
president for, first, a cement company based
in Mexico and New York and, second, an
international hotel and resorts company
with central offices in New York

Each was an education. Each was an arena in which I
discovered what it really means to follow a vision. The lessons were sometimes hard ones.

I continued learning the lesson that there is a price to
everything in life.

To succeed, I had to be willing to go where the opportunities were, which meant places far from home and
family. I haven't always been present for my parents during the hard times or the good times, except over the
phone. Especially early on in my career, that distance
was a source of much loneliness. Much later, when I was
more established in my career, more successful, it
became easier to set my own terms and call the shots
myself. So for a family birthday, an anniversary, I could
announce I was going back home for a couple of days of

celebration, pack up my laptop, and work from there.

I learned that solitude and isolation often came with being the first or only woman or the first and only Hispanic in the positions I held.

The real, overt influences of being the only woman or only Hispanic didn't become obvious until I took my first business jobs and entered corporate life. Even when I had earned my MBA and had several key positions under my belt, business meetings and conversations tended always to turn toward culture and sex. I was often faced with situations that unfortunately are common for women of all backgrounds, even today. I'd become the organization's unofficial spokesperson for all women or all Hispanics since often I was the only one around.

Many times, I had to explain that I was actually the person responsible for a project and not the administrative assistant. I often had to report to and work with people who would not or could not offer open, honest, constructive feedback to a Hispanic woman. I needed to sell my capabilities and repeatedly justify why I was the best person for the job, even after I had been hired for it.

But in turn and over time, those experiences gave me insight into the roadblocks many employees encounter. When you have made it through many small workplace conversations and situations in which the perception of who you are can trump the reality of who you are—

and not in a good way—your sensitivity becomes finely tuned.

I learned that God's timing is not always our timing.

I had seen myself running a nonprofit organization somewhere in my forties, after a number of years in the business sector. It happened much earlier, when I was asked to accept the position at the Martin Luther King Center. So I was a little thrown off: *Okay, God, I'm ahead of my plan, and it's confusing.* I remember that confusion was such a central part of my prayers at the time. But it was a learning experience also.

I learned that when you follow a calling, you won't fail even when you fail. All things will work for your good and growth ultimately.

There's a term that fits here: *anointed*. When you are anointed to be in a particular job, a line of work, you will be ready for it. More than that, you will be able to carry out your role better than others. You will be able to make things happen that no one else can.

When you're anointed, you bring with you not just intelligence or technical expertise or X years of experience. You also bring a set of qualities, a unique combination of the practical and the spiritual that didn't exist in that role before you came along. It's a special alignment of all that's needed to accomplish a task or a goal, and it's one that may not occur again. And it comes from being in the center of God's will for your life.

I've seen that happen in my own career. I have been able to accomplish things in some of my roles—build, align, restructure—that people before me had not been able to do. Was it because I brought to the role more innovation of thought or expertise or because I prayed more through situations? It was probably a combination of the two. And when I would take another position, the person who succeeded me wasn't always nearly as successful on a number of levels as I had been, even though I considered each of them to be far more intelligent than I was.

The Bible gives us examples of people attempting many things without success. But when the one person who was called showed up, it worked. I think that's the same in life. That strengthens my faith. That, to me, serves as hope.

You see, God does not call us to accomplish something and then sit back and watch us fail. One of the truths I've learned is that when He gives you a vision of which path to take, He has also equipped you or is in the process of equipping you to handle it. The end result has already been handled by Him if you stay on course.

A NUMBER OF PEOPLE have shared their stories with me, and I want to share them with you now. They speak of the sense of calling. They speak of being buoyed up by faith.

Tom is a scientist, a very smart and highly educated

man with a Ph.D. in chemical engineering and a long career track behind him in one company. Right out of graduate school, he took a job with a major international manufacturer in the chemical industry, and then he methodically worked his way up a corporate ladder. He describes that path:

"I moved from one plant to another. I started out in New Jersey, then [went on] to West Virginia, Maryland, Illinois, Pennsylvania, and Delaware. These were typically stints of six or so years at a time. My wife and I had two kids along the way, so there was a lot of buying a house, selling a house, exploring school districts, figuring out new commuting routines, and so on. I did that for almost thirty years."

There came a day when Tom's company announced plans to combine his division with another, and the new base would be headquartered in Texas. Some people in the division would be required to move. Some would probably be laid off. "It was one too much. I had a moment—or actually a long night—of epiphany. I call it my coming-to-Jesus moment. Aside from the fact that we weren't all that crazy about the idea of pulling up stakes yet again, I was asking myself, arguing with myself, whether this was what I was supposed to be doing with my one and only life. I was always passionate about science. In school, I thought I'd go into some kind of pure research field. As it developed, what I'd mostly been at for years was business and sales. Sticking with it was mostly about salary and equity."

Being unsettled turned out to be a blessing. "Probably if it wasn't that I might actually be out of a job soon, I wouldn't have started thinking these thoughts. There's that saying, 'When one door closes, another door opens.' I wondered what it could be, and if it somehow got me back in touch with my real passions."

Tom and his wife had a small time-share condo on the island of St. Croix, and they took a five-day vacation there. "On an impulse, I drove over one morning to the campus, the University of the Virgin Islands on St. Croix, and I asked for directions to the science department. I went in, had a wonderful talk with the head of the department for a couple of hours, got a tour. They needed chemistry and physics teachers, and basically I was told they'd hire me on the spot.

"I was thrilled! I felt washed over with an overwhelming sense of excitement and freedom. This was something I could do. Maybe was meant to do. My wife and I loved the islands, the kids were grown, we could envision a future along this radically different path."

He didn't immediately throw over all the old traces. They went back home to Delaware. Tom kept an eye on the restructuring process in his organization and what would be the likely outcome for him. There were money matters to consider—his pension, insurance issues, and possible severance. "But systematically, steadily," he says, "I began laying the groundwork for this other route. And it might not even be at that university but another somewhere in the islands where I would be needed. I felt life was aligning properly. The idea of introducing young people to aspects of science was tremendously exciting to me. I was making phone calls, figuring out some stuff, and there was a great sense of peace. The funny thing is that I never thought I had that courage. I had to be pushed before I thought of taking a leap of faith."

FOR ANOTHER MAN, faith came in what I mentioned at the beginning of this chapter as hanging in and hanging on. Benny comes from a Mexican family of businessmen. "All the men—my father, uncles, my brother, a couple of cousins—are in construction. They build malls. They're always out scouting property, making deals. They're very ambitious, driven people, very into money." Benny, on the other hand, is an artist, a portrait and landscape painter. "I love all the creative arts—theater, visual arts, fabric design. Everything I most love is everything my family can't stand," he says. "Or they just don't get it."

Benny graduated from a two-year program at a community college, and then joined his father and uncle in one of the family's real estate offices. That was the accepted plan for all those coming up in the younger generation.

He hated the work. "I didn't like the whole business, really. All you talked about was the business. They expected me to work nights, weekends; always hustle for new contacts, new properties; and get the best deals from suppliers."

After five years, "I still couldn't get my head into it. I felt like a robot. No soul." Benny says: "I've always considered myself a highly spiritual person, though I'm not religious in the usual way. But I respond to things of the spirit: great art, great beauty. I pray a lot. I think you get answers that way." At that point five years into his would-be career, he made a leap of faith.

"A friend of mine was opening up a beauty salon. Just a small shop, seven chairs. He was hiring people, and a lightbulb went off in my head: I could cut hair. Do something that was kind of mindless but satisfying. What's so bad about it? You talk to people, you make them look good. I work an eight-hour day, earn enough to support myself, go home, and leave my job behind—not have to think about it. Then maybe I could see if I had any real talent as a painter."

That lightbulb lit up six years ago, and Benny is still a hairdresser. He's also started to sell some of his paintings. "This was the perfect plan for me. As soon as I made the switch, I knew it was right. But I have to keep up my faith in that, because it hasn't been so easy. This is not prestigious work I'm doing. Not according to my family, not the day job and not the artwork. I get a lot of grief, a lot of ridicule from my family—not so much now anymore as in the beginning, but I still get comments. My father thinks I've blown it. But I know I'm okay."

*A*ND THEN THERE IS SHARON.

Sharon entered nursing school as a nineteen-year-old, got her degree, married immediately afterward, and never went into practice as a nurse. Her husband, Mack, was beginning a career in the banking business, and they set themselves up in a swell apartment in New York City. Sharon says: "Life seemed to move very fast. My adorable two boys were born right away, two years apart. Mack was having huge success in his work. We did a lot of entertaining. I got caught up in all that goes with having young children. I volunteered at their schools and took them around to all their activities and parties and whatnot."

Sharon and her husband eventually divorced. "The divorce became final on my fortieth birthday, and I took that as a sign of something or other. I was a good mother. I thought I had been a pretty good wife, generally. But I had that feeling, a feeling that I think probably a lot of women go through—the real Sharon had been put aside. The real Sharon, I thought, would have made a wonderful nurse."

So here's what Sharon did: She took a number of required courses and exams to reactivate her license. With her sons away at school, she pulled up stakes, returned to an area in northwestern Vermont where she'd spent a couple of summers as a child, and bought a small house. Then she signed on with a visiting nurse service.

"My territory is rural with pockets of deep poverty," she says. "I see many people who can't travel, can't get to health facilities. There's one woman I visit who is severely disabled by diabetes. She's had one leg amputated. The other evening, I was washing her as she lay in bed, her neck, under her arms, under her breasts. She told me it was so difficult for her to keep herself clean, and she thanked me. And I felt in the center of my universe. I felt I was the one person on the planet who was meant to be in that tiny room with that woman that night helping her keep clean."

*T*HERE IS NOTHING like the feeling of waking up and saying, "I know I am in the center of God's will for my life." It doesn't mean that you like all the immediate circumstances and surroundings. I can think of times when I have headed off to work with thoughts running a mile a minute through my mind—all the things that need to happen, all the problems that must be resolved, all the issues I'm going to have to face. But in the center is the peace of knowing this is where I'm supposed to be. The storm may be all around me, but I am in the calm eye of the storm.

When you wake up, do you have that inner peace that passes all understanding? Are you in the center of what you were created to do at that moment? That's the peace so many people are looking for. Some search for it their whole lives.

There is nothing like it. You can't buy it. Nobody can give it to you. And I believe you don't find it unless you take that first step to reach out to God and trust in His purpose. That's the source.

So here's the outline of my
FAITH–BASED ROAD MAP:

- Give God control.
- Keep moving forward, even when you don't have all the answers.
- Start over, if that's what is required.
- Fight discouragement, without and within—pray.
- Hold on to the vision. Listen for your calling and His voice.

TWO

Prayerfulness

The Conversation with No "Amen"

$\mathcal{I}$ REACH OUT TO GOD over and over again, in what I call the conversation with no end. Prayerfulness is the second principle of the Spirit-led career and life.

Focus on God and His Presence

One morning it was difficult to focus on anything but the unpleasant day I knew was ahead of me at work—meetings, phone calls, the politics, the people. I felt my energy zapped before I even started, as if someone had hit the Slow Motion button on life. With every step and turn I took to get ready to leave the house, I let out a sigh.

The drive to my office was no easier. My thoughts pushed me deeper into the black hole: *Why am I doing this? What on earth is going on? Do I really want to keep at it? Why? Who cares about the money? Maybe I'm not supposed to be in this job anymore. The stuff going on at the office isn't fair. It's not right. I'm tired of dealing with it.* By the time I had parked the car, I had sunk into a state of numbness and apathy.

That wasn't the first time I'd started a day like that in my career. And as on those other occasions, when I made it into the office I threw myself behind my desk, hung my head, and did the only thing I could muster enough energy for. I prayed. *God, if you don't come and do something with what I am feeling right now, I'm not going to make it today. I really need your touch. I need you to speak to me.*

On this particular occasion, a couple of hours later, after I had settled into the work at hand, I received an e-mail from my friend Gwen. It read:

> *Ana, I've been thinking about you all morning. I thought you'd like this message a friend sent me earlier:*
>
> *"Do you feel like you are groping in the dark? Why not explore the manufacturer's manual? "You guide me with your counsel. . . . Whom have I in heaven except you? My flesh and my heart may fail, but God is the strength of my heart. . . ."*

I sat up straight, and I experienced the warm, knowing feeling that had become familiar to me over the years. I smiled, the kind of smile you get when you've just had a letter from a longtime friend who reminds you of a special time and place you shared, of a bond that lasts. On my bleak morning, God broke through the reality of my circumstances and my inability to look beyond the moment. He reminded me that He was there, even though my focus was off and my heart was heavy. He heard my prayer and answered in a way I could hear at that moment.

So often throughout my career—when a task was horrendous or a situation was way beyond what I believed I could handle—He has tapped my shoulder and reminded me that when I pray, He answers. In my first corporate job, years ago, I had no idea how I was going to accomplish what those folks wanted from me. There I was, having just accepted a regional position, and I'd never been to any of the states that comprised my area. I'd never traveled. I remember thinking, *How am I ever going to pull this off?* And I sat at my desk and prayed, *God, if you don't come, I don't know what's going to happen here. I'm surely going to fail.*

He came. I didn't fail. I grew into the job and I thrived. But it took a lot of prayer. I learned then, and all along the path, that when we pray, He comes.

So HOW DO WE PRAY? Is there a right and a wrong way? Is it something you have to learn, or are you just good at it or not so good at it?

From my own experiences, and from talking to friends about their prayer life and how to lead it, I know this much: Prayer isn't always so easy. We can put it off or forget. We can be distracted. Sometimes we worry about what to say. Praying doesn't come as naturally as exchanging pleasant comments with a neighbor we bump into on the street. Of course, living a Spirit-led life isn't always so easy either.

At the simplest level, I would say that whenever you bend your knee and incline your ear to God in faith, you can't go too wrong. It always strengthens the bond. And it will indeed get easier.

Ask for Guidance

There are prayers of beseeching, when we're asking for help. There are prayers of praise, when we're giving thanks.

Throughout this book, you will see or perhaps have already noticed, I talk a lot about my frequent conversations with God as I've gone about my career. Many of those conversations have been asking for a "zap," an infusion right then and there, as on that morning when I felt I was groping in the dark as I sat at my desk in need of His touch.

In many other conversations, I've tried to learn His will for me when I'm faced with making a difficult job decision. Sometimes I have been completely baffled by doors that seem to be opening that don't make sense and I'm not sure what it's all about. And sometimes, I've been fighting disturbing feelings about a particular move, and I desperately need guidance. Guidance has always come.

Listen for God's Voice

Several years ago, I was being courted for a position as executive vice president at a major entertainment company, reporting directly to the chairperson. As the courtship went on, I had a number of meetings and interviews with some of the presidents within the organization. This was a big job. It would represent a major career move for me personally, in an exciting line of work.

From the start, however, even before the first interview, I was uneasy about the whole thing. I remember saying to my husband, "There's something that's not settling for me in this, and I don't know what it is. I'm just not at peace with any of it, for some reason." I found myself caught up in an *um, eh, maybe* attitude. I always know when I'm in the zone that tells me, *Ah, this could be a God thing.* I wasn't feeling that; I was not in the zone.

Still, I never miss an opportunity to meet new people and sit with them and talk, because you never know where those connections may lead. After the first round of meetings, I was starting to feel more comfortable about what my role would be in the company and what would be expected from me. But yet the sense of peace was not present. "Keep praying about it," my husband said. "You'll know."

One evening I sat in our prayer room at home and said, *God, I don't want to be anywhere that you do not have destined for me to be, no matter how great and sexy and phenomenal the opportunity sounds. For some reason, I feel no peace about this job, and I don't even know if my pursuing it is your will for me. But I'm going to do the legwork and see how far that takes me. And if this is not a step you want for me, if this is not where I need to be, please do something to close this door. If the door stays open, I'll assume it's where I am intended to go. And whatever is causing this unease that I'm feeling, help me figure it out.*

That was my prayer. I prayed it more than once after that evening, because I knew from my experiences along the path that when you're outside the umbrella of God's purpose and will, there's no peace, there's no success, there's nothing good.

The hiring process with the company moved forward over several months. I was the candidate of choice, the recruiter kept assuring me; no other possibilities were on the table. Then suddenly one day, the company called, informed me that another candidate had emerged, pretty much out of left field, I gathered, and—so sorry—that person had just been hired. I was not being offered the job.

I was thrilled. *Okay, I thought, the door has closed.* I had my answer.

I still don't know exactly what it was about the position that bothered me and gave me a lack of peace. I just sensed it wasn't for me. God confirmed it. And once it was confirmed, I really did not even care to find out how it all had happened. I just knew I had received my answer, and I was at peace with that.

You do get to a point in your spiritual relationship with God that you do just know. You stop trying to analyze and intellectualize and talk yourself into or out of whatever the issue is. You simply have faith that your unsettled feelings and lack of peace are a warning mechanism. I think of it this way: You're driving in your car and a little engine light comes on. Maybe a bulb is malfunctioning or maybe it's something more serious and the light is warning you about it. You're not sure. But you trust that if the light's on, you should at least take that as a warning and do something about it—check it out, get to the garage. You can't quite put your finger on the problem, but the message is real.

God sends messages. When you have a relationship with Him, God is big enough to stop you in your tracks and permit situations around you that will bring to an end whatever is going on. Or, on the other hand, He permits situations that point you on the path and tell you, *Yes, this is the way.* At other stages in my career, particular doors have just swung open, and not ones I was looking for necessarily. Each time I have prayed: *Lord, I don't know what this is all about, but I'm going to do my part. I'm going to do research on the company, I'm going to show up for the interview, and I'm going to give it my all. And I know you will do your part. I need you to either confirm this for me or to take this away.*

Whether the doors have opened or closed, He has never failed me.

Offer Thanks and Praise

Starting with a thankful heart will never lead you wrong, even when you don't feel all that thankful. There are days—we all have them—that we wake up thinking, *Oh no, I've got to go to work, the last thing I want to do,* and on those days I immediately force myself to stop and change the thoughts in my head. I say instead, *God, thank you for this house, for my husband, for my parents, for my clothes; thank you for the fact that I have a job that allows me to provide for myself and my family.* It's good to be specific in that way, to put a name to those people and blessings that we have. When I run down the list of what I have been given—even though my first reaction of the day is not thanksgiving—how can I not express my gratitude?

Offering thanks is really giving praise, and there's more than one way to do that.

A woman who spends a lot of hours riding buses to get to her job turns to the words of the Bible. May is a nanny, a daytime babysitter to two young children of a working career couple. She is a single mother, with two young children of her own who are cared for by their grandmother while May is at her job. Her life is not easy.

"I think it is strange that I must leave my babies to care for another woman's babies, and I think it is sad that I am away from home so much. I take two buses to get to work and two buses back. While I am riding, I have my Bible."

She began her practice by reading a Proverb a day, reading it over and over and thinking about the meaning. In a month, she'd read through the thirty-one Proverbs, and she turned to the Psalms. "The Psalms are beautiful," May says, "so many of them about praising God. When I read the words, I also am moving my lips. I do not say them out loud, because that would be annoying to people or they'd look at me. But to me, this feels like offering a prayer."

Prayer is a discipline and an act of intention. Like any discipline, you get better at it the more you do it. Think of it as exercising your spiritual muscles. I'm a runner, or at least I used to be. Now I am really a jogger. A long time ago I ran in several marathons. When I haven't run for a while, I can't just go out one day and start pounding down the road with all my old stamina and strength. It's just not there, and I've got to get back in training, little by little.

It's the same with prayer. I have been training myself in a robust prayer life for many years, but if I let the conversation slide—too little time, too much activity, too heavy a workload—I've lost something. The spiritual muscle needs to be built up again. And while we dally, He waits.

Prayer does not come easily, because it is not entirely natural for us to be prayerful. It's not in our genetic make-up. If it was easy and natural to lean on God, this would be Eden. So I want to share some ideas on how to get past the hurdle and weave this principle into the fabric of your working days.

Practice: Have a Conversation with No Amen

"I don't know what to say."

That's what a friend told me about her attempts to pray, and that's a feeling many people have. We get caught up in the words and become self-conscious. But just as there is in each of us an instinct for God, the God-shaped vacuum we long to fill, I believe there is also an instinct for prayer. Acting on the instinct takes attention and effort.

It's a discipline to have a conversation with someone when you might not be in the mood to talk or you feel awkward. So it might require consciously bending your personality and character and routine in that direction, deciding to make it a habit to set aside a few minutes every morning when you wake up just to talk. What you say doesn't have to be all that complicated or sophisticated, just honest words from the heart. Writer Anne Lamott once said that her favorite prayers are "Help me God, help me God, help me God" and "Thank you God, thank you God, thank you God."

But praying also means listening, sitting quietly and trying to hear. Prayer isn't a one-way conversation, after all. It's a dialogue. When you're talking, you're not really listening, and the act of being still takes practice also.

We all come under the attack of mental distractions, noise distractions, not being able to focus because of this or that. As I've mentioned, we have a prayer room in our house. In reality, my prayer room is anywhere I am at the moment, anywhere and anytime I feel the need to stop, slow down, and direct my thoughts to God. But at times, especially when I've felt removed, I do make a point to sit quietly in the prayer room. And all I might say is *Lord, here I am. You know my voice. Forgive me that I haven't spent more time with you. I don't know what to say. Because you live inside me, I need you to rise up and pray through me.* Approaching God in childlike honesty is never a mistake. Then be still and listen.

Sometimes I'll sit in my prayer room and sing a song that I used to sing when I was a younger Christian or that we sing in church. Singing to God is a form of prayer and worship. It's making a willful decision to put all else aside, focus on God, and get into a frame of heart to have the dialogue. Singing is a way to begin to get your heart in the game. I also come from a church tradition in which, before anything, there's singing. Interestingly, in the Bible, when Israel went into battle, often it was the singers who led, not the soldiers. The singers called down the presence of God.

Practicing this is also a reminder that prayer, like a relationship with God, is about surrender. *Talk to me, lead me, show me where you want me to go, and even if I don't always understand, I trust in what you have in mind for me.*

Surrendering can alter your sights, as I've said, but it doesn't always mysteriously improve your circumstances. Life is still there, and some of the days are going to be humdrum and drab, or ones you face with dread. But some days will be filled with events or people who will pump you up, make you feel on top and confident of your direction. That's when you need to surrender, again and again, and that's where prayer comes in. Surrendering to God goes against our very human instincts. We like to feel like we're the ones running the show. And it's often when things are going great on the job—when we're really digging in to the fast track and career success and visions of riches ahead— that we can so easily slip away from genuine prayerfulness.

Abigail, a woman who calls herself a spiritual person,

has worked for more than twenty years in retailing. Abigail started right out of college as an assistant buyer in a small women's specialty store in Maryland and moved her way through increasingly big jobs to her current one, as an executive in a major New York department store. Abigail described her path and some developments that reawakened her understanding of what it means to follow a Spirit-led career:

"I always adored retailing. It was the one area I wanted to move into right from school on, and I was so lucky to keep getting good spots. Well, lucky, yes, but also blessed, and also, I worked like a dog. I put in the hours. I learned the ropes. And I've always been big on prayer, and I just knew and trusted that I was doing what I should be doing.

"With the New York job, I was really hitting my stride. From the start, I felt this was my heyday. At one point, two of us were given the assignment of redesigning, completely rethinking the cosmetics, perfume, and personal beauty products department. This was the major revenue producer for the floor. I had a vision for how the whole thing would work, and I started counting on this to be a very big feather in my cap; definitely a promotion; definitely getting into the serious money personally."

For the better part of a year, Abigail says, "there was huge jockeying for position between this other person and me. I was getting extremely competitive, determined to be on top of everything and micromanage every detail. And here's where prayer comes in, and it wasn't a good thing at that time. I found myself praying every night, at the end of one of these crazy days, that God would cause a specific thing to happen. Literally, I was praying, 'I need to get approvals tomorrow on that plan, so please, let me find that memo on my desk.' I was praying that a meeting would go in my favor or I'd get a phone call I was waiting for. I was trying to micromanage God, I guess you could say."

She heard herself, she said, and didn't like what she was hearing. "I had the experience of surrendering to God, many years ago, and it was extraordinary, the feeling of releasing myself and trusting in His will. But what I learned lately is that one extraordinary experience doesn't take care of things forever. You have to have that conversation, the right conversation, over and over. You have to remind yourself what having faith in God's will is all about, and you have to practice it." She had to get her "prayer life back on track," she says. "And I was able to do that, and with it came a sense of ease that whichever way things turned out at work, it was okay. I knew I had done my best job, I'd put my passion and experience and commitment into it. The rest was up to God, and it would be okay."

That really is a positive challenge. We all have things we want, some of them desperately. We all may say in our conversations with God, *I need this* or *I need that*. They can be huge, well-intentioned requests, like to make a sick child well or to end the suffering of an old friend, or they might be tiny requests that seem so important in the moment, like wanting to see that approval memo in the in-box the next morning. The key is to remember to surrender. We often want to play both our role and God's, and we can't. I can only do my part, and then I must trust in Him for the rest. He has a plan for everyone else as well.

Join with Others

We have heard a lot in recent years about prayer, or prayer sessions, in the workplace—from the highest levels of government to the pregame locker room of pro football players to businesses that start the day with organized prayer groups. The one-on-one form of prayer we have been talking about here is what it takes to develop an intimate relationship with God to the point that you know Him well enough to see His will for you. When the relationship deepens, you will start finding another area of prayer opening up to you—praying with others. If the results are better when you pray in your own personal, private, even idiosyncratic way, then that's what it takes for you, and that is all right.

I've gained strength both from my private prayer times and from praying with other believers. It has often been the case when I've struggled with deep personal matters that a close friend from church has called and said, "You know, when I was praying yesterday, you came to mind, and I began praying for you. I had it so heavy on my spirit that you were going through something difficult and you needed prayer."

That's the essence of spiritual community. If you believe that God is omniscient and omnipotent and you invite Him to participate in your life, He comes with all His powers, so He has the ability to instill in the thoughts of another believer that you are someone to pray for. Or to instill in your thoughts that a friend is going through hard times and needs your prayers. Of course, you will not always have that intimate bond or sharing with everyone simply because you attend the same church.

But you do know when there's a connection with a particular person. And it's usually confirmed through events such as I described above—the phone call from my church friend, the e-mail at work. There's no way they could have known that at those moments I was troubled and needed prayer. There's no human way to have that knowledge; it comes only through the inspiration of God.

*H*ERE ARE SOME WAYS people of faith have met the challenge:

Jenna, a woman who grew up in a religious home, went to a religious school, and turned away from all things religious in her late teens, says: "Any kind of praying I heard or did as a kid began to seem totally artificial. We'd sit around the table at dinner and we had to join hands, and somebody said, 'Bless us, O Lord, for these thy gifts which we are about to receive,' and so on and so forth. It was just words. When I was very little, my grandmother told me that every night when I went to bed, I had to say, 'Now I lay me down to sleep, I pray the Lord my soul to keep. And if I die before I wake, I pray the Lord my soul to take.' So that terrified me, naturally, thinking I could die overnight, and of course I prayed that little prayer over and over. In the morning, there was another prayer: 'Lord in heaven, hear those who are praying to you now,' and so on. Everything ended with *amen*, which I thought was particularly meaningless.

"I gave it all up when I gave up going to church or believing in all the stuff my parents and the church told me I should believe."

She is now thirty-five. Jenna says: "A few years ago, for some unknown reason, I began to like the old prayers and I started taking them up again. I even say that childlike bedtime prayer now. Church is not for me. Religion is not for me. But I found comfort and actually a point in the routine of directing my mind at those certain times of the day beyond myself. It's a good habit. It feels like a good way to start the day and end the day."

*R*AMON, WHO WORKS AS AN ORDERLY in a hospital, says: "A few years ago I decided to learn how to meditate. A friend of mine was seriously into meditating, and she used to talk about how terrific it was. You lose your ego. You're at one with the universe, things like that.

"I see a lot of unhappiness on my job. People are very sick and getting painful treatments. Then there are also a lot of worried relatives that come with the patients. I take all this with me when I leave work, and I was looking for something to ease my mind.

"Well, that was the toughest thing I ever tried. The more I tried to relax my brain, the faster my brain started going. I never did get good at it, but I liked the idea of saying a sound over and over to get calm and get rid of the outside world. Almost a little trick you can play on your mind. I thought that could be a way to pray.

"I'm not very good with the idea of having a conversation with God. I can't talk to him like you'd talk to anybody. For me, prayer is about praising him. So since the meditating wasn't working and I found it tough just to talk to him, I've made it a point to memorize Bible passages, and I say them in my mind. My thing is, I get up early and spend about thirty minutes in the gym that's in my apartment building, usually on the treadmill. I recite one of the passages I've memorized. I also recorded passages on a mini cassette recorder, and I listen to those and think about the words while I'm exercising."

$\mathcal{O}$NE WOMAN, a computer programmer, looks forward to the hour or so in the evening when she's home from work and preparing dinner for her family. Helen says: "I used to put the news on TV while I was cooking. Now, instead, I try to bend my mind toward godly things. I love cooking, I love the whole process because it's sensuous— the smells, the colors of fresh vegetables, the feel of the water running over my hands. I try to have a prayerful or meditative attitude while I'm moving about the kitchen. I think about how blessed I am to have my home, my family, wonderful foods that we can eat. I think of how amazing and what a gift it is to have this astonishing abundance in my life. I concentrate on these blessings. How can I not be grateful?"

$\mathcal{D}$O WHAT WORKS: whatever it takes—anything that helps you break through, anything that keeps the line of communication open from your end.

I have learned that when we seek the face of God through prayer, we will find it. I have never once said, *God, I need you to meet me here*, and He did not in some way show up.

These are the principles of
PRAYERFULNESS:

- Focus on God and His presence.

- Offer thanks and praise.

- Ask for guidance.

- Listen for God's voice.

- Practice: have a conversation with no amen; pray without ceasing.

- Join with others.

THREE

Humility

The Mighty Power of a Humble Spirit

HUMILITY HAS A LOWLY REPUTATION. Humility suggests not putting yourself forward, keeping a low profile, or displaying an aw-shucks attitude about your accomplishments, yourself, and your life. It's a quality that's not usually mentioned as necessary for success in the workplace.

But I am convinced that humility is a key principle in a Spirit-led career. At its core is the understanding that my purpose comes from God. I am able to do what I do because of His guidance and because I have put to good use whatever talents and intelligence and opportunities He has given me. In fact, humility goes hand in hand with a healthy sense of self-awareness.

Demonstrating genuine humility is good for business. You recognize that you don't have all the answers, and you turn to people who can provide some of them. Humility is acknowledging a mistake when you've made one, and then trying to learn something from it. It's being open to different points of view. It's understanding that if you are in a leadership position, you get the best from people not by pulling rank but instead by making it safe for others to speak their part and contribute. And sometimes it's battling back feelings of superiority to those around you and meeting people where they are.

Acting out of humility promotes trust. It encourages wise and dynamic risk-taking. It draws people to you and makes them want to work with you. And you know what? You feel good about yourself and you feel God's purpose in a greater degree when you walk with a humble spirit through your working life.

Know What You Don't Know
and Ask for Help

Merced, a financial analyst, tells a funny but not-so-funny story about herself and about what happens when you can't admit that you don't know the answer. When she began graduate school, she moved away from home for the first time and shared an apartment with a roommate she found through the university. "My roommate knew people in the city, and she was nice about including me in her plans.

One evening I went with her to a friend's place for dinner. For the first course, everybody got an artichoke.

"I had never had an artichoke before. Didn't have a clue what to do with it. So I was trying to watch what the others were doing, sort of surreptitiously, and my friend noticed me sitting there strangely, and said, 'Hey, Merced, do you know how to eat one of these?' Instead of saying, 'As a matter of fact, funny you should ask—I don't,' I said, 'Of course I do. I just don't really like artichokes.' So right there, I created an awkward moment for the hostess, who got up and removed my plate and apologized, and of course no apology was called for. And I made myself sound like a child with no manners. Probably those people realized anyway that I didn't know what to do with an artichoke, so I was doubly embarrassed for the rest of the evening."

The artichoke event, she says, taught her this: "First, if you pretend to know something you don't know, you dig yourself in a hole that maybe you can't get out of, and you also feel like a fake. Second, you can lose out on learning something new or a better way of doing things."

Scripture says: "Pride goes before destruction, and a haughty spirit before a fall. Better to be of a humble spirit than to divide the spoil with the proud" (New King James Version, Proverb 16:18–19).

In business, you may be able to fake it for a little while, but not for long without being out of a job. But go further.

76

Step up and announce yourself as in need of more information. Admitting you don't have every answer is a sign of humility. It is also smart. You do, often, learn new ways or better ways.

I must confess that I fail the humility test quite a lot; sometimes it feels as if it's every time I open my mouth. Personality is part of it, and we are all acquainted with the attitude: "Here's what I think. Oh, you don't think so? Well, too bad for you." Not necessarily in those words, but you get the ugly picture. I always have to be more prayerful and mindful of what I say and how I say it. One of the lessons I've learned is to invite people into the thought process: "This is the direction I'm thinking we should move in. If it's the wrong direction or if anyone has a better idea, let me know. We'll figure out the best way."

At times, no matter what your role or level in an organization, there's also a need to say, "I'm sorry." And there's real strength in that—and respect to be earned.

I was in a meeting with a number of people, discussing strategic plans for expanding our business reach in a certain area. One young man began sharing his idea, which I thought was a pretty good one, though his proposed execution of it wasn't the best, and I said so. For the remainder of the meeting, I noticed he didn't talk again. I didn't feel then that I'd shut him down, but looking back, I realized that that was what I had done, probably in part because

I outranked him. In expressing my reservations, I wasn't sufficiently mindful of the fact that I was a vice president and he was a manager and that my comments were being aired in front of a large group of other people, which was uncomfortable for him. So it wasn't surprising that he clammed up. And maybe that was our loss; maybe he had other ideas behind his initial one that we all could have heard about—worthwhile ideas.

Later that day, I went up to the floor he worked on, up to his cubicle, and asked if he had a minute. Sitting on the edge of his desk, I said, "I noticed you got quiet in the meeting this morning, and maybe that was because it sounded like I was criticizing you in front of all those folks. If that's what caused you to stop sharing your ideas and participating, I just wanted to come by and say I'm sorry, because that was not my intention."

He was clearly pleased, and maybe a little taken aback by the fact that I was sitting there apologizing. He did share the rest of his idea with me. Then I was able to point out why his execution would not work, by taking the time to explain other pieces of the puzzle that weren't necessarily evident to him. In a leadership role, you must recognize that you see aspects of a situation that people sitting on other branches of the tree cannot, and are often working with more information than they are.

There's a graceful, gracious way of assuming a teaching role at work. I had not been gracious during that meeting, but I made an attempt to repair the damage later, as best as I could. Not only was that the right thing to do but it also had an obvious payoff.

The longer you work with a group of people, the more they start trusting one another and the more comfortable you will be about getting feedback when you ask for it. Initially, when you start working with people, they and you are still getting to know one another, maybe guarding their words. But you do get to a point at which they realize, *Okay, I gave her feedback, I spoke my peace, and there were no negative repercussions because of it.*

That's another message I try to convey to the people who work with me, and it comes from humility and a humble spirit: "I might have greater expertise or a bigger title, and I might have more information than you do on some issues, but I am far from perfect. And when my style for whatever reasons isn't working or I'm not listening well enough, let me know. I have blind spots; I mess up sometimes. I don't have all the answers. I'm only as good as the team we've built together. And every now and then, we will probably owe each other an apology."

You must pursue humility consistently. I'm still working on getting there. But I'd say that I have at least started on the journey. It helps to remember that your organization is partly rating you as a leader on your ability to put together a great team. If you can do that—assemble a group of people with different qualities and skill sets that together comprise something extremely strong—you can get much more done.

Do the Small Things as if They're Just as Important as the Big Things

A woman remembered her earliest job experiences as an intern in a suburban TV studio in Texas. "I came in with an attitude, I'd have to admit," says Frances. "I was going to work there for maybe a year, get the credit on my résumé, move on to a more important slot at a more important studio. Oh yeah, I was seeing myself as an on-air reporter six or seven years down the road, and right now I'd put in my time, pay my dues at this hick way station. There was a lot of stuff I believed was totally beneath me. I let things slide when I thought they weren't important or worth my effort."

As the weeks passed, Frances began noticing how the studio manager went about his job. "This man really wore all the hats. It was his responsibility to supervise me and the others on our minuscule staff and basically to ensure that our programming went off fairly smoothly. We had a limited broadcasting range, and we didn't do anything too exciting. But he paid attention to the details, and he let us know that they mattered—that the small stuff should be taken care of with attention and intelligence, because it all added up to the final result."

He was a strong manager, she says, "no pushover. He'd let me know, in a constructive way, if I had sloughed off on an assignment, and how I should approach it next time. But there was nothing arrogant about him, no self-important airs of being a big, bossy fish in this tiny little pond. He didn't consider that any task was beneath him. On many occasions, when the rest of us were occupied or people were out of the studio, I'd see him taking on some of the grunt work—filing the fact sheets, even packing up the trash for pickup."

From his example and direction, Frances says, she learned that "you don't get from here to there, not really, if you don't take the here seriously and do it thoroughly and competently. You've got to get off your high horse, if that's your problem. That was certainly mine for a while."

Looking down the road, having a career plan or goals, is smart, always keeping in mind that God may have a different time frame for you and that there are limitations to any human vision. But when you keep a humble spirit, you realize that doing small things well is one key to accomplishing bigger things down the road.

Meet People Where They Are

A lot of business discussions and relationship-building takes place outside the office, during corporate retreats, holiday parties, golf outings, and other socializing events. It's a fact, people are more likely to do business and work more cohesively as a team when they enjoy a certain comfort level with their colleagues. Like it or not, some level of socializing with coworkers is sometimes part of the interpersonal aspect of the workplace, and while it goes on, many ideas are developed and a lot of business does in fact get done. These events often can require humility, as I have learned, sometimes the hard way.

Early in my career, in some of my first jobs, I was often the only woman on the team. Today, corporate weekend functions held at hotels or club venues are more geared to a mixed group. After the business meetings or the think tank sessions are over, people can separate and pursue their interests—maybe playing a little tennis, working out at the gym, or getting a massage in the spa. There's less of a mold you have to fit into. Back when I got started, there were outings and functions that the team—meaning men, since I was the only woman around—assumed I would not be interested in and so would not invite me to join—golf, hunting, and deep-sea fishing, for example.

In no way, shape, or form did I believe those men were picking such activities in an effort to alienate me or leave me out. At least I chose not to think that. They were the majority, so they got to decide, and it was for me to say okay or not. But I quickly realized that in those golfing or hunting settings, colleagues were getting to know one another, talking business, and developing bonds that translated into the work environment. I knew that when they returned to the office, they'd have established a relationship of a more personal nature, one that I hadn't been around to build along with them. And that left me somewhat out of the loop. It worked to my detriment on the job, and so I made a point of inviting myself into the loop.

I remember a team-building retreat organized around a quail shoot at a hunting lodge deep in the Alabama woods. I was included, along with a departmental assistant who was invited as an afterthought so that I would not be the only woman in the company of six men. She and I shared a room in a rather large, chilly log cabin in the middle of nowhere.

Believe it or not, I found myself learning to use a 12-gauge pump shotgun while walking around the woods. The weather turned stormy, and we all hunkered down inside. A game of poker got under way, and I gained another skill I hadn't had before. All the while, there was talk of business. As we were looking at our cards, making our moves, someone would say, "Whatever happened with that legislator we contacted last month?" or "When we get back to the office, let's take another look at those figures."

Was it the best weekend I ever had? Did I come back and say, "Wow, what a great time?" No. But I wasn't offended by this all-boys choice of outing. They picked the playing field, and it made sense for me to go along. I saw the wisdom of adapting to a situation in which my personal preferences and interests were not primary, and I got to know some decent colleagues better and to engage more fully in our business.

It is always a challenge to balance a good career opportunity with the reality of being in a lonely place. Over time—and I have had to practice this—it became easier to step up and say, "Hey, can we do something else next time? Maybe instead of hunting we might plan a team dinner at the country club," knowing all the while that my suggestion might be unpopular. But meeting people where they are also affords an opportunity now and then to give them insight into where you are.

Along my career path, there was another lesson: At holiday dinners and parties, when spouses were included, I realized it was smart to talk mainly to my male colleagues' wives. They were curious, naturally, about this female with whom their husbands worked, maybe slightly threatened by this woman who spent more time with their husbands during the day than they did. Being single, I often didn't have a whole lot in common with them. My life consisted of working, traveling on business, and going to church. (Actually, it wasn't much of a life in some ways!) So I'd find myself in a conversation with someone's wife about schools and summer camps, things I had little clue about and scant interest in. But to discuss the business trip I was on with her husband would not have been appropriate or welcomed.

Did I enjoy it? Not really. Not only because I was not yet a mom myself but also because I had nothing to contribute to conversations on the topics they were interested in. While I really wanted to be at the other end of the room with my colleagues discussing "office stuff," I realized that the effort that I put into getting to know their significant others ultimately paid off in trust and respect at work. That's another way I learned to meet people where they're at. And I made a lot of mistakes in the process.

But the bigger lesson was this one, and it's a lesson in humility: Before anything else, we are all in the business of being human. We are all of value in God's eyes; we each have a purpose. And we each have our stories to tell. When I start believing my own press too much, when I'm in danger of feeling a little superior to what's going on around me, I remember that I am flawed, and that a humble spirit shows understanding and compassion.

Sometimes I've had to apply those lessons to my appearance. Should you be able to dress how you want, follow your own distinctive drummer? Perhaps. Is that the wisest, most humble path? Not always.

Here's an example.

I have curly hair. I love my curls, but I blow my hair straight for work and work-related events 99 percent of the time. The point is, it's not always appropriate to have my hair looking somewhat wild, and the way curls sit on my head, they look wild. It doesn't communicate what I need to communicate; it distracts. Now, I can go one of two ways with that. My attitude could be *This is who I am—like it or not; people should pay attention to what I'm saying and what I can do.* Or it could be *I do look a little more polished and professional when I tame the hair, and once people start getting to know me, then I'll venture out.* I've done that in the office: Once I was familiar with a place and my colleagues were familiar with me, I "let down my hair," and I heard, "Oh, wow, you've got really curly hair." But they already knew me, so it wasn't a distracting factor. It was just a new aspect of Ana. Don't get so caught up in your rights that humility flies out the window.

One of my favorite comments by Dr. Martin Luther King is this: "Laws may be changed, but real reform will not come about until the hearts of men are convinced." In some of the less welcome aspects of a career path—the times I might prefer being somewhere else, doing something else, looking another way—meeting people where they are is a kind of peaceful resistance, not in the sense of allowing myself to be molded by corporate America into what I am not but in continuing to be me, making adaptations that my common sense and prayers tell me are right and appropriate. In that way, what's on the inside—who I am—has the best chance of becoming apparent to the world.

Give a Little Praise When Praise Is Due

The companion of saying "I'm sorry" is probably saying "thank you" from time to time. None of us hears "thank you" often enough. In the workplace, maybe we don't hear it at all, and that's a shame.

For example, take Steve, a statistician.

He was part of a highly specialized team conducting a task analysis on related job positions in a major communications company. The study took a year to complete and produced a 150-page report. It included clear recommendations for change in several areas, which were in fact implemented by the organization and made for a business that was better run and more profitable.

Steve says this: "I was decently paid—we all were; no gripes on that score—but I ended up with my nose kind of out of joint. This was the job we were supposed to do, and I certainly was not looking for a gold star or a medal of commendation. But when the whole thing was over, I expected, I guess, some kind of pat on the back, some acknowledgment that we'd done well. I think it would have been a nice gesture if the chief operating officer just came around and shook our hands, let's say, and voiced a little understanding of what it took in terms of time and brain power and talent to get that study done. A little 'Thanks, guys.' "

As humans, we want to feel loved. As employees, we

want to know we're valued and appreciated. Raises and promotions are terrific, of course, and a sign that we're doing what we're hired for. But we'd also like the occasional accolade, the "Good job; nice work; well done" from the organizations or the bosses we work for.

Can you ask for them? I say yes, absolutely. Is that compatible with humility, as I'm talking about it here as a principle of a Spirit-led career? I think it is.

Most companies and organizations do have systems and processes set up to review employee performance. If they're conducted well, such sessions are encouraging. But too often, they can sound like "needs improvement" rundowns. If your manager is not gracious in providing positive feedback, maybe that's time to ask for examples of where he or she feels you have done a good job. I would even recommend asking for a list of some of the strengths demonstrated in your performance.

Not all managers are capable of providing good feedback—and not necessarily because they are dissatisfied with your work or your ability to add value but simply because in their own career they probably missed out on training about having such conversations. In some cases, managers themselves aren't receiving the reinforcement they need from their superiors to pass along to their teams.

You won't always get what you want or hear what you'd like to hear. But you should expect a "Good job; well done" now and then, and I believe you're right to ask for it.

Anyone in a leadership position really should remember the powerful impact of sending forth a little praise and thanks to their teams every so often. A midlevel manager in a retailing field says: "In my former job, when you saw an e-mail in your in-box from the boss, you dreaded opening it, because it was always something negative, and at times, it was something actually nasty. In this job, an e-mail from my boss doesn't start my stomach churning automatically, because she'll send a message off and on just saying, 'Appreciated all the long hours you folks put in last week.' The other day we had a message: 'Thanks for braving the blizzard and making it in this morning.' It's a small kindness that makes you feel good about working for this place."

Ask for What You're Worth

Can you have a humble spirit and still ask for what you're worth in dollars? That's a hard one. Women, in particular, seem to have a tough time negotiating for themselves, whether it's for a pay raise or a promotion or a starting salary and compensation when interviewing for a new job.

One woman says this: "I have a lot of trouble being assertive without sounding in my own ears like I'm pushy or aggressive." She worked in a nonprofit organization in the arts field, and every so often she was given a raise. "I was in that company for six years," Kathryn says, "and these increments in my pay were barely noticeable, not even keeping up with cost-of-living increases. This was a small place, and the director would come around with a slip of paper with my new salary marked on it and say, 'Well, Kathryn, it's not much, but like we used to say in Missouri, it's better than a poke in the eye with a sharp stick.' So I felt I had to chuckle at that, to look like a good sport. And then of course I'd start thinking I should probably be glad to get anything at all, and maybe I'm not worth more than this anyway."

It's easy to lose steam, to second-guess yourself and question your value. It's also easy to ignore steps you can take on your own behalf. The first step should be an objective, clear-sighted exploration of compensation in your field and at your level.

Over the course of my career, I have learned how to place an accurate value on my talents in the marketplace and to ask for it. That can be tough. It's hard sometimes to stick to your guns.

At one point, I was approached by a company that had heard about my work and expertise and wanted to recruit me. I had a good job, but I was interested in this new possibility, so I did some exploring: I researched the organization, talked to others in similar positions, got an idea of comparable salaries, and checked out apartment prices in the city I'd have to move to. Then I pursued the spiritual answer, through my conversations with God. My research and my prayers left me at peace that if I made the decision to accept the new job, it was the right one. And I knew what I wanted. I figured there was no reason those people should listen to me and agree to my demands, but the demands were sensible and fair. So I figured I had nothing to lose.

Early in the discussions, my potential new boss asked, "What kind of compensation package do we have to come up with to get you to make the move and work for us?" I gave him specifics—salary, bonuses. And I added, "This is what it will take for me to leave my current job and make the move to your organization. I have weighed everything out, and this is what it looks like for me."

"I don't see a problem" was his reply.

More talks, more interviews, everyone was happy, and yes, I was the person they wanted. Their human resources representative tracked me down on a business trip in San Antonio, Texas, and presented me with the company's offer, which was less than what I had proposed. "Take some time to think about it," the representative said, "and get back to us with your answer." My reply, on the phone, was, "Okay, I've thought about it, and my answer is no." Of course, I was more diplomatic. I was polite, I thanked the company for considering me, but I said that regrettably, I'd have to decline the offer.

The company executives were surprised, to say the

least. Nobody, they told me, had ever turned them down before. I said, "Well, then you're going to need a little time to think about what you want to do about this. I outlined what compensation I expected, and said the basis of how I had formulated that figure."

Was their package a good one? Yes. Was it what I knew I was worth and the industry standard? No. Was it easy to turn the offer down? No, it was not, and in fact I got an earful from people close to me about my decision. I remember calling my parents, telling them that the organization had offered me the job, and they were thrilled that this Fortune 500 global company wanted to hire me.

My mother asked, "What did you say?" And I explained to her that I had told them no, I wanted X, and they came back with Y, so my answer was "Sorry, I cannot accept." My mother's response: "Who do you think you are? That kind of money with a company like that, who are you to turn it down?"

We talked some more, I described my point of view, and after we hung up, I thought, *Oh brother. I really don't need this "Who do you think you are?" conversation right now.* For a split second, I considered calling that company back and saying, "Sorry, I'm on a business trip; I wasn't thinking clearly. Of course I'll accept your offer." But after the split second, I knew I had to follow my heart.

Some people would call it self-confidence on my part. Others might deem it hubris. I would call it God confi-

dence. I saw my decision as believing that what I was asking for was in keeping with His purpose for me. It's starting
with the notion *I'm just another human being. I'm not as terrific as my ego often tells me I am. On the other hand, I know
that God has led me here. I know what I have to offer, and after
careful thought and prayer, I have put a price on my value to an
organization.* When you start from that place of Spirit, then
you are able to approach negotiations with a clear mind.

Many adults whose immigrant parents arrived in a new
country with little or nothing and consider themselves
fortunate to earn any kind of living can find it difficult to
explain their career moves. Those from the older generation would never think of leaving a good job or turning
down a good offer. For that generation, making such moves
sounds reckless and prideful: *Who do you think you are?*
When someone so close takes you to task in that way, of course
it can throw your own conviction right out the window.
You think, *If the rest of the world attempts to undercut me,
tells me I can't, won't the people who love me stand with me
and tell me I can?* Outside obstacles will be there, so you
want at least your inner circle to be on your side. But
you're not always going to get your wish. And then what do
you do?

It's about the doors that open, I believe, moving
through them and pulling others with you. After watching
my decisions over the years, my mother has come to me
and said, "You know, I see the faith you have in stepping

out when you know God has something for you. You don't compromise and you don't take less." And that, in turn, has filled me with greater faith.

By the way, that company called back, met my compensation requirements, and offered me the job. I went on to relocate and work with them, and I walked further along my journey.

When you are changing jobs or are coming up for review in your organization, your ability to negotiate with conviction, after having done your homework and made sure you are within reasonable limits for the industry and your level of expertise, is also an indication to any employer of your ability to negotiate on the company's behalf. If you can make a strong case for yourself, chances are good that you will do the same for the company.

In the business environment, it is entirely possible to be both a godly person and savvy about what you should be paid for your experience and expertise. It's not pushy if you prepare yourself and know what you're talking about. I always encourage people whom I mentor to size up their market worth. What are other companies paying people in similar roles with similar track records? What you may feel you should be paid and what is actually a standard for what you do or the field you are heading into might be two different things. Gather information. If you're up for salary review and you are confident that your work has matched or exceeded expectations according to your job description, marshal evidence of your good performance. Go armed with a fact-based presentation of why your outstanding accomplishments should be reflected in your compensation.

And then I would add: Put money in its proper place in your life. Scripture tells us it's the love of money that is the root of all evil, not money in and of itself. It's our relationship to money, our thoughts about it and what we do with it that determines whether it wields a good versus an evil influence in our particular circumstances. Both good and evil can happen to the wealthy as well as the poor. In fact, anything we love to the extent that it comes before God in our lives will be the root of evil.

Be Empathetic—
Treat Everyone Like a Customer

I was a cashier at Kmart while I was in high school, and the company ran a promotion called the blue-light special. Select items on sale were loaded in a cart, the cart was put at the beginning of one checkout aisle, and a flashing blue light told everyone which aisle that was. The blue-light special always seemed to land at my register, which meant general chaos as dozens of shoppers lined up at my aisle.

One day when the chaos was especially insane, a woman I'd rung up insisted I had shortchanged her by a penny. It was 8:30 at night, the store was closing in thirty minutes, and I was exhausted and not in the mood to deal with this person or her penny. Dealing with her would involve recounting my whole cash register drawer while a line of people were waiting. We went back and forth—she's showing me her receipt; I'm saying she has that penny in her hand and should just count out her change again if she doesn't mind, and "You have got to be kidding me!" Eventually, we settled the matter. She found the penny among her change. As she left, she said, "You know, you could have handled this with a much better attitude." I said, "Have a nice evening."

My dad was waiting to pick me up after work, as he always did, and I stormed into the car in a blank funk. He asked what had happened. I started griping about the woman who, after putting me through all that nonsense about one cent, wondered why I had "an attitude."

My dad said something like this: "You know what? No matter what happens, the customer is always right. If she believed you shortchanged her a penny, then it was your job to count it out for her again and show her that she was mistaken, and to do that with a spirit that represents that store well. And if you don't like your job so much that you're taking it out on the people who come through, the people who are paying your hourly wage because they're shopping there, then find another job."

Well, while you can say my father showed little sympathy for my mood, I learned a big lesson there. He was right. I didn't want to be a cashier at Kmart, and I didn't have a humble disposition with that difficult woman at my register. He was right that if I was not dealing with the customers properly, if I disliked what I was doing to the point of damaging the store's reputation, I needed to find something else to do. It was nobody else's fault that at that time the only job I could get was as a cashier at an hourly wage working with customers.

But I believe there might be a bigger lesson in this concept of the customer. Think of all the people you deal with in your workplace—the people on your level, the ones below you, and the ones above you on the organizational chart—as customers. You are interacting with each in a particular way for a particular end. In this case, the customer isn't necessarily always right. But he or she is a person who wants something, needs something, or has a point of view or information to get across. When you look at the situation that way, you almost naturally become more empathetic. Empathy goes along with humility.

Stop, Back Up, and Rethink

The opposite of humility is an inflated pride—belief in and assurance of one's own worth and superiority. Sometimes that's justified; sometimes it's excessive. In either case, the consequences of pride can appear in different ways depending on our personality. When passive-aggressive people feel under attack or underappreciated, they may retaliate when it's least expected, in the least likely and perhaps most damaging manner. With a personality like mine, the reaction is immediate, predictable, and explosive: "You're going to get it from me right here and now, both barrels." Then when I'm done firing my barrels, I'm left sitting there thinking to myself that that was hardly a good testimony to the Spirit-led life and career and that I need to apologize yet again. I remember a couple of such instances.

A team I once led and I came up with a clear direction for a project—specific plans, specific executions, a timetable—and everyone was in agreement. Two months into it, one member of the team—out of the blue—decided to add a little twist to his assigned role, and that in turn threw a little twist into what others were doing. But nobody let me know. So as I was reporting the progress to my superiors in the organization, I was operating under inaccurate assumptions. I learned this when one of those superiors called and said, "Will you update me on that project? Because I just heard . . . ," and went on to describe those new turns I knew nothing about. I sat there feeling my pride and ego and fury rising up. I was blindsided.

On another occasion, I learned that my boss had given

an assignment to one of my colleagues—when I was the person running the department. I felt pride, ego, and fury rising up again.

In each of those cases, and at other times on my career journey, I followed up immediately with an e-mail or a phone call, demanding explanations: "What's going on here? Why am I hearing from X about what's happening? This is not what we agreed to. If we're changing gears, somebody should at least have the decency to inform me. This was completely out of line." The frustration was justified. The pride was understandable. Yes, someone took too many liberties, and as a result I was left in the dark and answering questions about issues I knew nothing about. But I heard my own voice and I saw my own words sent from my computer to a coworker's computer, and I recognized the combative tone. I was on the attack.

Needless to say, that's never good or productive. At the practical level, such reactions inevitably suck you into verbal combat or turf warfare and the real issues are not handled properly. At the spiritual level, those behaviors can never be justified. One of the things I know is that in the eyes of God, I'm held accountable for my actions and reactions. Pride comes before downfall, we're told, and a haughty spirit before a fall. Every time I react out of pride or haughtiness because I believe truth and justice are on my side, the result is disappointing. And I'm off the spiritual path. When we come from pride or ego in life, that will never create a positive outcome. It just won't. A bad tree will never bear good fruit.

So this is why I'm learning—and relearning and relearning—to slow down, back up, take a deep breath. Think. Consider what I most wish to achieve and what actions will get me there.

For the backing up, you need a lot of humility.

Respect Expertise When and Where You Find It

"I cannot believe some of the kids who are coming into this business," says Maureen, who works for a film-editing studio in the advertising field. "First off, they think they know it all. Nothing they have to learn. Second, they don't see why they should have to put in a full day's work in the office. They think that's so old-fashioned. They can do work stuff at home is the attitude, or run their little laptops at a Starbucks and get the job done there. Third, they expect to be heading up the place in two years. They have expectations about how fast they can move up that are completely unreasonable.

"The arrogance just amazes me. I was in a meeting the other day and we were going over some accounts, and this fellow started, 'In my experience,' and then he went on to give his very inflated opinion about something or other.

And I'm sitting there thinking, *In your experience? You're like two years out of college, you're sitting around a table with some folks who've been in advertising for twenty-five years and more, and you're talking to us about your experience?*"

Maureen says she understands that a generation of younger employees has grown up differently from the old guard. "These are kids who always had computers, the Internet, computer games, MTV. They don't get the hierarchy and the structures because their world has always been global, networked, and their youth prized and exalted in the media. Their point of reference is completely different. The way they view life and culture and the world is different. Maybe for the only time in history there is this melding of two very different generations in the workforce."

She doesn't think that's all so bad. "These young people, a lot of them, don't come with some of the old hang-ups or limitations or stereotypes. They're kind of rewriting the way work is done, and that can be exciting. I can learn something from them. But they can learn something from me too. That's the element that got dropped. There's no humility."

I know what she's talking about. One of the developments I have seen over my career is a loss of respect for the expertise individuals can bring to an area of work. Everyone's now dispensable. It's true. I always work as if I am dispensable, because in fact I am. The company I'm with can hire someone else with my skills to do what I'm doing. But this is where I believe calling comes in, or what I described earlier as the spiritual notion of anointing. Ten people, let's say, know enough to run a department, but maybe only one has the spiritual calling to be in that company in that job at that time. Only one has the combination of qualities to implement outcomes with unique success. Only one was so blessed and anointed.

Being bright goes a long way. So does youth. But there is no substitute for experience, no substitute for having gone through processes that lead to insight and intuition in a work setting. Gaining experience takes time. Rarely would I—even now—use a phrase like "in my experience..." in a meeting. I'm always aware that there's still someone with more experience than me.

*L*ET ME SHARE one more story with you, this from a woman who says she ran smack into the whole idea of humility—and what it meant and how she had to acquire a good dose of it.

Jackie was the travel editor on a national magazine. She held the job for fifteen years, and she loved it. "I thought I had the best job in the world," she says. "I mean, just imagine. There I am in Greece, getting information for a feature on hotels and restaurants and beaches on the islands of Sámos and Kos. Maybe a month after that I'm looking at Roman ruins in Malta. Or I'm in Patagonia. And I am not paying for any of this!"

Five years ago the magazine Jackie worked for went through a major shakeup. The travel section would be eliminated, with only an occasional article about travel to be supplied in the future by someone off-staff. Jackie no longer had a job. With a lot of knowledge and experience to offer, she decided to set up her own business, becoming a consultant to tourism industries in foreign countries and a coordinator of tours for vacationers.

"I thought I knew what I was doing," she says. "And I was totally unprepared for what turned out to be a 180-degree, upside-down shift in the way I worked—a shift in my life, really. On the magazine, I was the one who was wooed. It was obviously great publicity to get a mention in the magazine, and all kinds of people and organizations and outfits were constantly cozying up to me. I was the buyer, and they were out to sell me something. And I got quite a sense of my own importance over those years, how I could pretty much make someone's day by including them in a feature or story.

"So when I launched my little business, I was coming from that place mentally and spiritually and the tables got turned. Now I was selling something I was trying to get other people to buy. And a lot of time at the beginning, they weren't buying. It took me a while and a lot of falling flat to realize I tended to blow people off if they didn't immediately get how terrific I was. I got very huffy very quickly. If somebody didn't return my call, forget about that guy.

"I had to learn about humility, and not phony pretend humility but the real thing. I reached out to a woman who was running a similar kind of business and who'd been doing it for a long time, and she gave me all kinds of great advice. She had a wonderful, generous attitude about that. I made a point of following up with people I'd approached, sending them clippings or news items I thought they'd like. Instead of sitting at my computer and waiting for the world to come to me, I met these people in their offices or shops. We'd sit and talk. I tried to understand better what they needed, what they were really after. I sent notes or left messages thanking them for giving me their time."

Jackie says it all added up to a lesson in the power of a humble spirit. Her business is doing well.

Remember That God Has Shown Us the Way to Humility

There is in every human being a part that seeks God, that reaches toward relationship with Him. The problem is, however, our very human instinct to say, "I believe in God, but unless I can find that relationship on my terms, it must not be God." To me, it goes back to humility and being able to bow your knee and bend your neck, and say, "It's not about me; it's about You. God."

At work, maybe that message is "It's not about me; it's about all of us."

At the beginning of this chapter, I noted that humility didn't rank high among the qualities needed for career success, not according to the advice we've heard from some of the big honchos of the business world. But there's evidence that things are changing, as more organizations come to appreciate a model of business management that's being called "servant leadership." A national TV news magazine led off a discussion with the heading "Can humility and faith be good for business? Was Jesus the ultimate CEO?" He washed the feet of his disciples, of course, in the most powerful scriptural demonstration of humility. Today, many corporate leaders are saying that spiritual values, absent of religious dogma—including acknowledging what you don't know, asking for answers, and offering appreciation—makes for the best business.

My rules for
PRACTICING HUMILITY:

- Know what you don't know and ask for help.

- Do the small things as if they're just as important as the big things.

- Meet people where they are.

- Give a little praise when praise is due.

- Be empathetic—treat everyone like a customer.

- Stop, back up, and rethink.

- Respect expertise when and where you find it.

- Remember that God has shown us the way to humility.

FOUR

Integrity

Doing All as unto God

*I*NTEGRITY CAN BE THOUGHT OF as what you do when you think nobody's looking. Being honest, having a sure sense of right and wrong and going for the right, acknowledging personal mistakes, showing compassion—these can be real challenges in the workplace because it's often both easy and tempting to slide under the radar. Lots of times it's true: Nobody is looking. Nobody will know whether you acted with integrity.

At the beginning of the day, when my feet first hit the floor, the only ones there are me and God. At the end of the day, it's the same. He's watching, even when the people in your world might not be. So what are you going to do with that? Start from the notion of doing all as unto God, and the answer is clear.

Draw Your Moral Line in the Sand

In a previous chapter I talked about meeting people where they are. For me, that has sometimes meant joining the boys—my only colleagues at the time—on hunting or fishing retreats.

In some jobs, when again I was the only woman on a team of eight or nine, we'd gather for national meetings every several months. After the talk sessions, the group would go out to dinner and then end the day at a sports bar. I've never been into bar scenes. But still, it is sometimes necessary to attend dinner and then leave. I still do that. I want to let coworkers know that I'm part of the group, but I don't need to participate in what can devolve into heavy drinking or raucous behavior. It's just not for me. I don't buy into the idea that when you're away on a semibusiness, semisocial event, there is a kind of parenthesis in time—as if it doesn't quite count, as if God doesn't see. It's a fine line to walk.

One woman describes her office as "an environment of lighthearted moral depravity." Angela works for a graphics design company. "My title is administrative assistant to the president. I do routine paperwork. I don't get involved in the more creative areas. This is fine. I don't have any huge desire to do other things. The job is good for me because it pays fairly well, I can walk to work, and it's strictly nine to five. I'm very involved in a lot of volunteer activities on my own, so I just want to go to the office, do my work, and then I'm out of there."

Not long after taking the job, she became aware of the socializing going on among her coworkers. "There's a lot of playing around—actually, sleeping around. My boss is a young guy, late thirties, very cute, not married. My first month there, I went out twice after work with the others, because this seemed to be the routine. There's a bar right downstairs, and a mix of people from the office would stop off there for a drink, and then several of them go on to do some barhopping. I didn't want to look like a little snob, so I figured I'd join them for a glass of wine. On the second evening, I was sort of startled to see my boss and Merri, another assistant, hanging all over each other fooling around. I suddenly realized, *Whoa—those two have some kind of sexual thing going on.*"

Over time, Angela witnessed small scenes and heard bits of information around the office that told her that what she'd seen wasn't an isolated moment. "My thought was *The boss isn't married, Merri isn't married, nobody's cheating on anybody.* And I don't see anything wrong with getting involved with somebody you work with. It happens all the time, of course. But I think you should be discreet, and those two weren't. Then I began to realize that a number of people were playing fast and loose around that place.

"One of them, Theo, is a vice president. He's also late thirties, and this man is married. His wife just had their second baby, and he's been carrying on an affair for the last two years with a woman who used to work in the o ffice. She shows up every now and then, and the two of them go off somewhere for the afternoon. I learned this from a coworker who loves dishing out all the dirt about people."

The fooling around was distasteful to Angela. "I don't like it. I don't get guys like Theo. But the atmosphere is condoned, and it filters down from the top. This is a pri-vately owned small company. The president, my boss, is the son of the founder. Nobody has to account to anybody. So the questions for me were *Is this behavior so offensive to me that I shouldn't be here?* It was a sweet job, and I defi-nitely didn't want to leave, so I decided I had to deal with it in some way. *Staying here, am I sort of tarred with the same brush? How can I stay, make my feelings known in some way, and not hurt my relations with the boss and not come off sounding like a self-righteous prig?*"

Angela faced the challenge of drawing a moral line in the sand, being in an environment but not of it. That's a tough one. It goes right to the heart of living out the prin-ciple of integrity while living within a real workplace and getting a real job done. She says: "I adopted the notion of 'see no evil, hear no evil, speak no evil.' It's not hard to avoid the drinks after work and the barhopping. I always declined—good-naturedly—and after a while they stopped including me. Everybody got the idea that Angela just isn't much of a party girl. Maybe not a lot of fun, but that's okay. The harder part was turning off the gossip."

When her coworker Merri started to tell tales about what had gone on the night before or the latest about Theo and his girlfriend, Angela just smiled and said nothing. "That didn't entirely work, so finally I said something like 'Merri, you know, I think it's better if we don't get into this stuff. I'm a little uncomfortable hearing about it and it interferes with my relationship with the boss, so I'm sure you can appreciate my feelings here.' There's a little chill between us now, but I can live with that."

There usually are ways to handle tricky situations of this sort without sounding judgmental or getting on a soapbox for clean living and upright behavior. Your relationship with God is yours; God does not require you to wrench others onto it, and that never works anyway. But I do think that making your moral position clear through polite but determined behavior can have a ripple effect on those in the vicinity. Less dishing of the dirt probably makes for better productivity as well.

Have the Tough Conversations, for the Right Reasons

Acting with integrity sooner or later invariably draws you into difficult conversations, some you'd give anything to avoid.

When I was just starting out, some of the toughest conversations had to do with work I was asked to take on because of my gender and my cultural background. I became the de facto expert on women and Hispanics because I was the only one of either category there. So whenever issues arose around recruiting Hispanics or women or around the Hispanic market segment, people asked me to help. And this was great, because in a corporate setting you do want to get those "stretch" assignments and show that you can be versatile.

But often that would take up huge amounts of time. I remember several occasions when I had my own work and then added work that could have been the job of another person. That's when you have to operate with wisdom. *Do I want to blow the opportunity of being seen as someone who can do more? No. Do I want to jeopardize my current responsibilities? Absolutely not; my current responsibilities are what I was actually hired for. Am I doing the work of maybe two full-time employees? I am. So how do I express my concerns?*

One company I worked for had had business operations in Cuba before the revolution. Now, the Cuban government was reaching out through religious organizations to persuade my firm to continue funneling in some of our products as part of humanitarian aid. My phone rang, and I became part of a task force involved in this peripheral area that had nothing to do with my job. It made sense, because I did have the contacts in South Florida from my lobbying days. But I realized I had to have the tough conversation with my bosses. That involved saying, essentially, "I can take on these additional assignments, but they are detracting from my ability to do what I was hired for. I can't continue to do my job and also be on two- or three-hour conference calls several days a week. What exactly do you want my role to be here? Is there any way these efforts can be put on hold? Is there any way another individual can handle them?" Or an alternative would be to keep doing both, and doing neither well or to the best of your ability—would that be right?

Those are tough conversations. You've got to be a little bold.

You can also be a part of leadership and still run into the need for a tough conversation—and fail to take the bull by the horns.

Here's an example of putting off the inevitable and making matters worse:

Phyllis worked for a jewelry-exporting company. The hard conversation that wasn't happening involved a young assistant in her department. Phyllis says: "There were three of us appraisers and there was Ann, our assistant. Very bright and a recent Harvard graduate. Why that child ever took that job, I have no idea. She aspired to write fiction. No interest in our business, which was all right, but the problem was she did not take care of the business.

"Her work, which was routine and fairly boring, piled

up. Ann was often on the phone in personal conversations. She was an emotional young woman, given to histrionic outbursts. Half her desk was taken over by short stories she was apparently in the process of trying to write. Before long, it was clear she had to go."

Phyllis had been with the company for less time than her two colleagues had, so she felt that the confrontation with the delinquent Ann should properly be handled by one of them. "We all agreed that she wasn't working out. But my two associates had completely different approaches to the mess. Lee was simply furious at Ann and barely spoke to her. She would often slam the door to her office so she wouldn't have to hear Ann on the phone. I gather she believed this was conveying a message of disapproval. Hazel, on the other hand, adopted a maternal attitude. She thought Ann was a troubled young woman who didn't get along with her mother, which apparently was the case, and Hazel was going to provide the soothing encouragement Ann needed to bring her around to becoming a functioning member of the team. So Ann and Hazel were often closeted in Hazel's office, with Ann pouring out her dreary tales."

Nothing changed. Phyllis decided that the ball was in her court, by default. "I took Ann out to lunch. After some pleasant chat, I got to the point. I told her the job was not working out and that the position did not seem to suit her. She stared at me. Then, for some odd reason, I asked her if she'd ever considered a teaching career; I thought she'd enjoy that. To my horror, she burst out crying."

Eventually, the deed was done. All three associates sat down with their assistant, and Ann exited the company.

Terminating an employee is never easy. It doesn't get easier, however, as time goes on, and in fact interpersonal working relationships can become more muddled. Phyllis says: "This young woman was in the job for one year, which was about eleven months longer than she should have been. We all suffered. It came from a failure of will to do the hard thing."

This type of tough conversation is a stumbling block for most of us. For me, an "I calls 'em as I sees 'em" type, it is still absolutely gut-wrenching to have discussions with people about how things are not working out, poor performance, and so on. No one enjoys wounding another human being who might be struggling through life stresses of some kind. I spend time in prayer before I have one of these necessary, unavoidable, hard conversations, so that I may do it with wisdom, justice, and integrity.

You won't always get it right. But look at Ecclesiastes: there's a time for everything—a time for war and a time for peace, a time to love and a time to hate. On a career path, there is a time to overlook issues and work with the person performing badly, and then there's a time to put an end to things.

Offer and Ask for Open and
Truthful Feedback

Feedback often creates more tough conversations. But good and useful work, I believe, gets derailed because people have trouble saying what they mean. Just blurting it out isn't as easy, and a number of issues can crop up.

Companies have become sensitive about the possibility of lawsuits. Everyone is on guard about what they say and whom they say it to. A man giving a man feedback is in a very different conversation than a man giving a woman feedback. In the man-to-woman scenario, he's probably not going to be as candid; he's likely to dance around issues. I've had conversations that finally prompted me to stop my colleague and say, "I'm sorry, it's probably me, but I'm not tracking with what it is you're trying to say. I know you've got an idea here that could potentially be of benefit to me, but I'm having difficulty understanding. What don't you just tell me what you're thinking, and we'll see how it all sorts out afterward?" Individuals sometimes try to be so cautious and politically correct that their message can be lost.

In a leadership meeting I attended, the discussion concerning review and succession planning came around to a man in a particular area. He was well regarded, but the group didn't sound 100 percent behind promoting him. One man finally came out with a reason. "Fred is a great guy, very smart," he said, "but his deportment is just not what it needs to be. He looks terrible. He doesn't dress right. The way he carries himself doesn't give a good impression."

Someone else around the table said, "Well, have you told him that?" And Fred's boss replied, "No, I've tried to suggest some things subtly. But how do you come out and talk to someone about the way he looks, the clothes he wears?" If Fred was never told that he didn't dress appropriately, his career would not advance, and the poor guy would probably have no clue why that wasn't happening. That's a no-win all around.

Eventually the conversation with Fred took place. In fact, the company offered to pay for a short-term program of coaching and training in the area of his perceived shortcomings. It all worked so well that changes for the better were even noted in Fred's performance.

Giving open and honest feedback to others about what's not working is, to me, a reflection of courtesy and compassion. It's resisting the very human instinct to brush a delicate subject under the rug, look the other way, or put it off.

Take Criticism as Well as Applause

Integrity includes owning your part—the good, the bad, and the ugly.

If you're given responsibilities, you must answer for the failures as well as the successes. Take the credit both when things go badly and when they go well. I have told my teams, "I'm not going to participate only in the successes. I also take responsibility when there are failures. And I'm fine with that, because that's my role. But that means that while I'm here to give you the accolades, I'm also here to tell you when something's going wrong, because we're in this together."

In fact, I have been thinking about this principle in recent years and have changed my thinking somewhat: When we succeed, we all succeed; when we fail, I'll stand up and take the brunt of the negative consequences. I'm finding that it is a lot better to handle things this way.

Do What You Said You'd Do
When You Said You'd Do It

Jenny left an office job to strike out on her own. She was feeling both wildly excited and hugely nervous. She says: "This is something I've wanted to try for years. I've always been good with my hands. I make door wreaths, dried flower arrangements, stenciled wrapping paper. A couple of years ago, I started making gift cards with leaf imprints on the front. All kinds of little things like that. I gave them as presents to my family and my girlfriends. Then I started to sell them to the [women] I worked with in the office, and I was actually getting some nice business.

"I had some savings built up. Then when my grandma died and left me some money, I said, 'Now or never.' I thought I could give myself a year and work at the crafts full time. My dream plan was to open up a tiny shop, maybe in the basement of my house."

She had a friend who encouraged her to take this entrepreneurial leap who had followed a similar path years earlier with success. "Scott had all kinds of information that I didn't. I knew where to get my materials, but there were details about marketing, packaging, maybe setting up a Web site and selling that way. He promised to help me with all that. And I know he wanted to. There wasn't any problem about competition between us, nothing like that. His work is completely different from mine. But he disappears on me for weeks at a time. He'll promise to send me some little piece of information, maybe a phone number or Internet address I need, and then he just doesn't."

Most frustrating, Jenny says, is the fact that her friend rarely responds to any voice mail or e-mail messages she leaves. "I made a little business plan for myself when I started this a year ago. Maybe that's too fancy a word for it, but I had a rough timetable. Scott gave me input on that. Now it's pretty annoying that the timetable is off because I can't reach him so often. Then he pops up, and I'll get an e-mail with some excuse about why he wasn't in touch. One time he said his sister was sick and he had to go back home to Oregon. Last month, he said his partner was very ill for a while. And you know, I thought he was lying about that. Anyway, it's just polite to answer an e-mail, even if you're just gonna say you don't have a lot of time right now."

It is impolite not to respond to business-related messages. When it happens repeatedly, it's not only impolite but also damaging to your reputation. Integrity on the job shows up in meeting your deadlines, returning phone calls, doing what you said you'd do when you said you'd do it. Jenny makes a good point: Even if you are unable to comply with someone's request—you don't have the information, you haven't had time to check out the matter or figure out the answers—at least keep in touch. Let the other person know that you're aware and on the job and that there'll be more later.

Unexpected things come up for all of us. The rest of life intrudes. People do get sick, but is a sick relative a genuine obstruction or a lame excuse?

Would you make excuses to God?

Make Sure That Your Yeses Mean Yes
and Your Nos Mean No

I've talked about knowing your value to a company—putting a price on your expertise and asking for what you're worth. When you are not offered what you're worth, or reasonable accommodations you ask for are not made, take action. Sticking to your guns shows integrity. You show a lack of integrity, I believe, when you back down or back off, and then maybe fume silently or issue vague threats that really have no teeth because you don't intend to do anything about them.

I'm thinking about a job I had earlier in my career. After being in that role for three years, I approached my boss to talk about my future in the company. I said something like this: "I've been successful; you've rated me highly among the rest of our national team, so you're obviously pleased with my work. Perhaps now I can start interviewing for other positions—maybe in our D.C. office, maybe abroad. I'm starting to get a strong desire to work in another country and use my foreign-language abilities."

He was amenable. I did begin interviewing within the company, and they liked me for a role in Buenos Aires. I was excited about that, but the possibility fell through when the organization ordered a freeze on all international positions. So I went back to my boss and asked if, at a minimum, I could move into our office in a neighboring city. It was a bigger, livelier city, and I thought it would give me more diversions when I wasn't working than the small town I was then in. His response: "Well, I'd like to, but I already used up my relocation budget on Jake in Texas."

Me: "What's Jake got going on? He already lives in the state; that's his primary market."

Boss: "Yes, but he's working out of Fort Worth and his wife and kids are in Houston, and he spends too much time away from them. So we're going to set him up in Houston."

Jake was not rated as well as I was in terms of work, by the way. So I looked at my boss and said, "Okay, I understand." By that I meant, "I get the message."

Fortunately, I had some other opportunities at the time and I had prayed about what my next steps should be if the response were as I thought it would be. I wrote out my resignation and sent it to my boss. His response was to get on a plane and fly back to my office with a copy of the resignation. Here's how that exchange went:

Boss: "What on earth is this?"

Me: "Oh, that's my resignation."

Boss: "You've got to be kidding me. There are dozens of people who would absolutely love the position you have here." (This isn't exactly what he said, but the exact wording should not be in print.)

Me: "Well, that makes me feel better. You won't be stuck with an empty desk for too long, then."

Boss: "Let's talk about it."

Me: "We have talked about it. For the last three months, we've discussed my career development. If you are telling me now that you can't find four thousand dollars in your budget to move me, then that's telling me the value I have here. And that's okay. We're at least clear, and we're on the same page."

I found another job in another organization. And the job that I left? It took the company nine months to fill it.

I feel strongly about this: Never threaten that you will leave. Don't talk about it. Threatening is counterproductive and decreases your credibility. You become known as simply a chronic malcontent, and that never gets you anywhere. Do everything needed and possible to make a situation right. Pray, pray, pray. Closing a door God opened and has not told you to close is not a good idea. But once you know the situation cannot be righted, it's time to pack your bags. Don't just talk the talk; sometimes you're right to walk.

I certainly don't mean to sound breezy, as if newer and better jobs are always just a phone call or two away. Or as if considerations such as career investment, family responsibilities, money problems—all that real-life stuff—don't come into the picture. But if you are plugging away endlessly under a cloud of misery and resentment, your ear is not tuned in to what God is speaking.

Especially in the corporate world, difficult issues come up repeatedly, and often in subtle or even nefarious ways. There are people who aren't going to support your efforts. Some won't get in your way, but neither are they about to help. There are the people who say they will support you but are working against you behind your back. Then there are the ones who don't support you and actively work against you.

Regardless of an individual's power to damage your position, remember that God is in control. He is bigger than the office bully. Even if that bully might like to do you harm, there is nothing he or she can do without God's approval. It's just that you have a daily nuisance in your life to combat. That's when I start praying: *God, are you allowing this for a reason? Or is this a sign that it's time for me to go? And what other door are you about to open?* This is a critical prayer. There are times when God allows us to go through difficult periods, for our growth, so it's important to know the difference. By the way, that boss who wouldn't relocate me? We're still friends, and he has told me that my career path since I left his company is proof that I made the right move.

Take a Stand for Honesty

Because I've worked in corporate relations for most of my career, I handle information and relationships external to the company. Sometimes I'm crafting messages that go out to the media, intended to present a positive picture for the organization. Often, I'm asked to supply statistics—numbers and figures. Almost always, there's one person in the place who says, "Couldn't we include these other numbers that would boost how we look in that area? Can't we count that over there as part of this over here?" I've learned to say no.

I am very clear: "I won't fudge numbers, I won't blur lines, and I won't lie. And if that's a problem, then we need to talk about exiting me right now. If you as my boss are going to override me, then you're going to fill out the document and you're going to sign it, but I cannot." I had expressed this part of my work ethic during an interview at one company and would often remind my boss of it.

Sometimes I'd hear: "Well, I'm sure our competitors do this kind of thing."

My reply: "I don't work for our competitors. I work for you unless you fire me for not doing this. If the company is going to handle this in this manner, somebody else can do the fudging, but I can't."

I wasn't always that bold! I got there over time. I eventually thought, *Whose bad side am I going to be on? Am I going*

*to get on God's bad side or my boss's bad side? Well, this man's
arms are too short to box with God, so I think he's on his own
here.* You don't have to be arrogant or "holier than thou" to
convey the idea that you don't lie for anybody.

Not everyone in a position of power, however, is going
to accept that explanation.

A man who works in a carpentry shop became aware of
practices he didn't like. "I do a little of the assembly stuff,"
Phil says, "but mostly my job is working with the suppliers
and keeping the records. The units we sell are basic,
nothing too fancy: kitchen cabinets, bookshelves, built-
in storage sections. The guys go out to the customer's
apartment—most of our jobs are in the city—take mea-
surements, build the piece in the shop, go back and install
it, print up an itemized list of supplies and labor, and bill
the customer."

The billing practices were what bothered him. "With
the hardware, you can use different grades of merchan-
dise. This would be hinges, brackets for sliding drawers,
things like that. Basically, there are the cheap varieties
and the better, more expensive varieties. Now, your aver-
age customer isn't going to know the difference. You don't
see these things on the surface; it's not cosmetic. And in
most cases, the cheap one and the pricey one are both
going to get the job done, though the pricey one is going to
do it a little more smoothly and probably last a little longer. So here's what's going on, in a nutshell: I order the

cheap one and bill the customer for the pricey one, per the boss's instructions."

Phil wrestled with his options. Should he speak up or keep his peace? "This kind of cheating goes against my principles," he says. "I did it because the boss told me to. But when I don't say anything, I figure I'm pretty much agreeing with what's happening. That was eating at me."

One day he approached his boss. "I tried to keep it real casual. I said something like 'You know, this overcharging, it doesn't sit right with me. I think we shouldn't be doing this,' and a couple of comments like that. He says, 'Don't bite the hand that feeds you, pal. You do what I tell you.'"

Phil is still wrestling with his thoughts. "I'm asking myself, suppose I can get out of this aspect of the work— somebody else handles it. I wouldn't feel so bad because I'm not the one out-and-out doing it. But I still know it's going on. So is that the same thing?"

This is a moral dilemma common in workplace scenarios of all kinds. What is your responsibility when you perceive wrong activities, though they don't directly involve you? This is something I struggle with. Is it my job to call out everything that I see? I don't necessarily believe that it is.

If I'm being asked to take an action that's immoral, illegal, or unethical, that violates the principles of my relationship with God, then I do have to do something about it. I have to have a say. It's my particular responsibility to perform my job with integrity. But I do not think I'm called on to be a whistle-blower on anything not morally or ethically correct. I might have to fill out that survey or give that interview or write that message, and to the extent that that's my job, I must be honest and truthful. But I don't have to go into some other department and nose around somebody else's job and point a finger.

I have voiced my opinion on things. When someone has been promoted, for example, I have at times expressed my conviction that his or her behaviors and actions don't line up with what we're trying to achieve as an organization. When I'm hiring a new team member, I convey this message: "If you engage in any behaviors that violate company policy, you will not have my support. Whether I think it's a good or bad policy, that's not for me to say. All of us who work here make the unspoken commitment to uphold the policies of the company, so that's what I will expect." What I don't do is assume the role of moral watchdog at large.

Fortunately, most major companies these days have codes of conduct employees must sign, and these are excellent vehicles for helping anyone out of the moral dilemma we're talking about here. A code of conduct is a binding document outlining, from A to Z, the ethical behaviors expected of employees. Typically, it says as well, "If you are asked to perform or are aware of any unethical or illegal activities in the office, you can report them anonymously at the following number at the following place." These ethics hotlines or committees on good corporate practices can be invaluable sources of help and advice.

Act with Empathy

It's human nature to resist change in a work environment, especially when the change is foisted on us without our input or agreement. Even if we don't resist, often we can feel anxious, unsettled, fearful, or resentful. Familiar routines and people make life comfortable. New ones come in, and things don't feel so safe anymore.

Change is inevitable. Workplaces rarely stay the same year after year. They can't, because that's not the profile of a modern, healthy environment. And change—maybe new management, new technology, new visions—can be energizing, exciting, and good for everyone. Often, however, what determines whether it's success or distress at a time of change is the human factor, the trickiest factor of all.

If you're the person in charge, the one who's handed the assignment of producing a certain result, your focus is on that goal and how to achieve it. That's when people's needs and vulnerabilities can be overlooked or given short shrift. A few bodies might get trampled on the way to the goal.

One woman describes major lessons she learned about acting with empathy, and they came when she accepted the position of executive director of a nonprofit organization. "I had always worked in corporate jobs before this," says Margot. "And those jobs were all very outcome oriented, not much thought given to the process. In this new spot, the board had a number of very clear objectives, and I was considered the best among several candidates to achieve those. So I walked in on day one, ready to work my miracles, and I came smack up against a 180-degree difference in the way things were done. The environment, the work approaches, the cultural perspectives—all this was in many ways completely counter to my experience.

"The people implementing the work of the organization were lovely people, with the attitude 'We do things our way here; we're not for profit. And my attitude was 'No, actually we're here to make a profit; it's how we use it that's different. We will be using the profit to turn it back into programs, whereas business companies hold on to it. So let's be clear that our role is to raise money to do the things that fulfill the mission of the organization.' My new staff wasn't taking this well.

"I learned that people who work in nonprofit tend to be more cause-oriented. They tend to say, 'I want to work here because I'm doing good for humanity. I'm working for the common good.' At the same time, these are still human beings. There's still 'he said/she said' stuff. There's

'I can do that better than you can.' There's 'I want to get ahead, I want more praise, I want more money.' They just want all that to happen while they're doing good.

"So this was interesting. I didn't find the behavior to be all that different from what goes on in corporate America; it just shows up differently. The ambition looks different. Someone's not performing well? That, too, looks different, because the conversation tends to be: 'Well, she's really such a nice and good person.' And I'm there saying, 'That's true, but it has nothing to do with her performance.'"

Her previous work, Margot says, had been about building and creating. "Here, I was actually dismantling, restructuring, moving about. I was taking something that people were used to doing in a certain way and saying, 'We're stopping that, we're shifting gears, and we're headed in this direction.'

"There was a lot of reeducation. Here's an example. Our two main contributors were corporations that worked on a January 1 to December 31 year-end financial program. They—reasonably—started budgeting for the next year in September, so it didn't make sense to call them in November about putting dollars in their budget for us for the following year. Their budget is all signed and sealed by that time.

"Now, my little nonprofit team had its year end in June. So they had been operating on a completely different cycle, and we were actually in danger of losing these contributors because we weren't paying attention to their needs and their schedule. And I came in and said, 'These companies don't care about our cycle. We need to see what time of the year is beneficial for them and works within their structure, and that's when we need to solicit them.' This threw everybody for a loop. There were many instances of this kind of thing."

She was working with a group of people who had based their worth on doing work a certain way, Margot says. She changed all the rules on them. She adds: "What does change do to people? It freaks them out! It makes them scared. They're thinking, 'What does this mean for me? What if I can't adapt to this new way of doing my job? What happens?' I wasn't sufficiently appreciative of that.

"I started out with a just-pull-up-your-socks-and-get-on-with-it approach. I had to teach myself to get into their heads and hearts and try to understand how all this felt for them. They were good people. They were doing good work for the betterment of the world. They were also human beings, and like all of us, [had] anxieties or weaknesses, hopes and dreams, ambitions, the whole ball of wax. I could be a kinder, more thoughtful, more empathetic person in the way I went about imposing the new expectations."

Empathy goes along with integrity. Especially if you are in a position of changing old practices and procedures, it's both kind and smart to uncover what people need to ease their way along. That might be temporary extra training or an open-door policy that encourages individuals to express their concerns. It might mean honoring elements of the past in small ways, such as keeping up the hallway bulletin board where everybody sticks up postcards from their vacations. Much of the time, I have discovered, employees feel calmer when they're given fuller information about both specific timetables and the bigger picture. Nobody wants to be in the dark. Empathy almost always leads to better communication.

*H*ERE'S A STORY of acting with integrity in difficult circumstances, in a hard life:

"I got into drinking, drugs, and I pretty much trashed my life. Before, I had a good job as a trainer in a gym, which is ironic when you think about it, considering what I did to my body later," says Eddie. "I was in that pit for eight years. If you knew me then, you'd have gotten out of my way fast. I had a kid with this girl I hung out with, and I disappeared on them. I picked up jobs here and there, so long as I could get paid off the books, so nobody could track me down for child support. I never had a regular place to live for years, but I didn't much care so long as I could get drunk. A real lowlife."

A year ago, Eddie made the decision to get clean. He

started going to Alcoholics Anonymous (AA) meetings on a daily basis and gave up alcohol and drugs. He got a job driving a cab for a car service. "You don't pull out of a life like that overnight," he says. "Maybe you never entirely do—I don't know. That remains to be seen. I'm trying to get a little money together and I'm thinking what I should do about this kid. The owner of the garage is a pretty decent guy. He's letting me sleep in the cab in the garage. That's hardly an ideal situation, but I don't have anyplace else to crash, not if I plan to stay clear of some of my former companions. One day at a time, as they say."

One of Eddie's fares was a young boy, about ten or eleven. The boy's mother had called the car service and requested a cab to pick up her son at an after-school program and drop him off at their home. "I deliver the kid, he pays me with a bunch of singles, and I immediately see that he's mixed a twenty-dollar bill in with the others, by accident. By the time I got back to the garage, the kid's mother had called my dispatcher and said she thought her son might have given the driver too much money; he was missing a twenty. So I played it out in my head. I could say to the dispatcher, 'No, I don't know anything about a twenty. The kid must have dropped it somewhere or it's in his book bag or something.' Who could prove it?"

Eddie didn't do that. He told the dispatcher he had the money, the boy had made a mistake, and they'd see that it was returned to him. He says, "I don't entirely buy the

AA line, but I've read the pamphlets. The part of needing to make a searching and fearless moral inventory of yourself—I agree with that. There's a lot of wrong stuff you can get away with in life and nobody knows. But you know and God knows, if you believe there's a God. For me, I think this turning over a new leaf, getting clean, it's not a thing I can do halfway. It's all or nothing."

Do all
AS UNTO GOD:

- Draw your moral line in the sand.
- Have the tough conversations, for the right reasons.
- Offer and ask for open and truthful feedback.
- Take criticism as well as applause.
- Do what you said you'd do when you said you'd do it.
- Make sure that your yeses mean yes and your nos mean no.
- Take a stand for honesty.
- Act with empathy.

FIVE

Forgiveness

Freeing the Bitter Spirit

To FORGIVE is almost always a conscious decision. Someone you work with has wronged you. Let's say that that individual is out to make you look bad or trying to undercut you or even get your job. Or maybe the dishonest or shabby behavior wasn't aimed at you but has had a negative impact on your effectiveness and your mood.

We all know the feelings. You are angry. Over and over again, you mull over the unfairness of what's going on or what happened. You tell yourself you've got to let it all go, you've got to move on. And that's when you discover just how difficult forgiveness can be. Your head is in the right place. Logic and life experience tell you that letting it go is the healthy and appropriate—and the spiritual—thing to do. But your heart and soul aren't anywhere near that place.

More than any other emotion, the anger and resentment that continue to bubble up when you can't forgive is what can turn a workplace toxic and, more importantly, what can make you toxic. You don't want to be there; you can't stand facing the person who has disappointed or betrayed you. You want to forgive, but it doesn't feel good or it's not really working. The trouble is, if you choose not to forgive or you simply can't do it, you create a kind of soul tie with your offender. You're stuck.

Then there's the other side of the coin—forgiving yourself when you've messed up. I know a lot about that. I know how hard it can be to give yourself a break, put your mistake in useful perspective, maybe learn from it and move forward.

Forgiveness on any level cannot be attained without God. He is the one with the power to change what's in our hearts, and He knows what a thorny challenge it is for us humans to act in the right direction.

There are productive ways to think through a difficult situation in which we have been hurt or have offended others, and then steps that lead to a good outcome. Forgiving people doesn't mean that we agree with their behavior. Neither does it mean you must continue to labor on in unpleasant circumstances. And if you're in a leadership position and faced with bad behavior from someone you're managing, restoring that person's effectiveness might be just as important as forgiving.

But for me, living out the principle of forgiveness in a Spirit-led career always starts in relationship with God.

Let Go and Let God:
Lay Down Your Rights

One time early in my career someone was trying to fire me, basically because she thought I wanted her job. I was just starting out, I needed the money, and I was completely baffled by her behavior. This woman was experienced, fifteen years my senior, and my supervisor. How could she think I was trying to replace her? I was pretty sure I hadn't given any signals to that end, because though I was a newcomer to the world of work, I already had my sights set on other areas entirely. This was not the organization in which I planned to dig in and move up over the long haul. I didn't want her job.

Knowing that the company was going through changes and that cuts were almost surely coming soon, I decided to take the bull by the horns. I said to my boss, "If my position is going to be affected, I'd appreciate knowing that." "Everything's fine," she said. "No need to worry, you have my guarantee." Something told me that she was not being honest. I was right. As I learned later, at the very moment she was assuring me that all was well, she was actually working behind the scenes to have my position eliminated as part of budget cuts in our department. I did a lot of praying after that conversation: *Lord, you know my circumstances, you know where I'm at, you know what I need, and if what I'm sensing is correct, you must fight battles that I'm not even aware of here. You either need to stop this or to find somewhere else for me to go.*

Two days later, I received a call from another organization that wanted to hire me. I was able to switch jobs, and the whole confrontation at my old job never came to pass. I was thankful that God intervened and was happy to move on.

However, I did harbor something in my heart against that woman, and the feelings were not going away. I remember in a prayer time at home saying: *I have to be honest with you* (as if He did not already know the truth; it was more that I had to come to know it myself). *I cannot forgive this person. What happened was wrong. It wasn't fair, it was completely unwarranted, and she didn't tell me the truth.* And a piece of scripture suddenly came to mind: "Freely you have received, freely give." I sat there for a moment thinking of this. *What have I been given freely? Well, I've been given forgiveness when I ask for it. I've been given mercy and grace.* So the words were telling me that these were gifts I'd received, though I had done nothing to deserve them. Now in the same way I was to give freely to another—perhaps undeserving—human being.

I sat there during my prayer time, and in my continuing conversation I admitted that I couldn't seem to find that ability to give freely, to forgive. I had been wronged, I said. Then I listened, and God's message to me was this: *Are you willing to lay down your right to be upset and angry? You have that choice. I can't take you there. First willingly lay it down, and then I will give you what you need.*

I told God that I was willing, but I just didn't feel it. It wasn't in my heart. And God said, *That's not for you to take care of. That's my part.*

Whenever the anger and resentment flared up, I'd pray. A couple of weeks later, I suddenly realized I no longer felt animosity toward that woman. I wasn't brooding about the situation, harping on it and rehashing it in my mind—what I should have said, what I could have done. It was over. I hadn't given her a second thought in some time.

Long story short—about a year and a half later, at a football party at a friend's house, I bumped into that old boss of mine. And what had happened? The organization did carry out a restructuring, and her job was the one eliminated. She'd been out of work for almost a year; she'd had to sell her house and move in with her brother. We talked, and she congratulated me on my new position. What I felt for her was sorrow. I spoke to God about her later, and all I could say was *Lord, have mercy on her.*

Looking back over the previous year and a half, I saw how He had kept his end of the bargain, changing my heart and putting forgiveness there. I was freed, I had been able to forgive and let it go, which I hadn't entirely realized until that chance meeting with my former boss. We weren't going to be friends, but I had nothing against her and certainly no feelings that losing her job was just retribution. Did I remember the events that transpired? Yes, but not with the emotion or sentiments that I had previously had. I do believe strongly, however, that you reap what you sow. That's what caused me to feel sorrow for her, because she planted the seeds that she was now reaping so unhappily herself.

Once you lay down your own weapons, once you have forgiveness in your heart, it also makes room for God to deal with that person, in whatever way that's going to happen. I like to think that for my old boss, His mercy would in the long run lead her into a relationship with Him.

After such an experience, you understand the importance of forgiveness. You understand what it means and how it plays out in real time.

Look for the Greater Purpose

Here's another story from my career path. This experience was more painful than the one I just described. It lasted a lot longer. The emotions it stirred up in me were harder to live with. And it taught me new lessons: about forgiveness, about God's timing, and about how getting the short end of the stick in the workplace can make you stronger in the end.

Over the space of a year in this position, I became the target of a pointed strategy not just to make my life miserable but also to undermine most of the things I was working on. This is not at all a rare occurrence in large organizations. You might have had a taste of it yourself. You are marginalized, excluded, and made to feel very uncomfortable in the hopes you will just quit. That's the endgame in mind, for whatever reason. Maybe what you were hired to do is no longer a company priority. Maybe a new management team wants to bring in its own people. From the standpoint of the organization, it's easier and, of course, cheaper if the out-of-favor employee just leaves quietly. Maybe you are not out of favor but perhaps someone wants to put another person in your role and management is not a part of the whole thing.

Regardless, in environments like any of these, tolerating the injustice of it all and the scheming that goes on is exhausting. You have done nothing wrong. Negative forces are at play that have no connection to your skills and talents or the efficiency with which you're doing your job. That's when you can get really stuck. That's when forgiveness and laying it down seem next to impossible.

I went through months of not receiving replies to my memos, months of being left out of meetings. Roadblocks were thrown up against any of my efforts to implement strategies. Adding to the discomfort, it was obvious to people around me what was happening, which made it embarrassing. My ego was involved. Some colleagues sympathized. One or two formerly friendly ones looked the other way when I went by.

I needed to stop churning about the situation. I needed to think clearly. And yet I just could not lay it down without looking over my shoulder the next day and picking it up all over again. I could feel rise up in me contempt for the spot I was in, contempt for the organization, for the people. And I became mired in the rightness, even the righteousness, of my emotions. Forgiveness was the last thing on my mind or in my heart.

One of the ways to live these principles is to allow yourself to be 150 percent honest with God. I can't stress enough that childlike honesty with Him. He already knows that you are unwilling or unable to let go of the bad situation. I remember my prayers during that bleak time: *I have been working in an environment that is so awful. You're God— you can blink and make this stop, but you're not. So if you're not, what is in this for me? What is it that I need to keep doing? What is my responsibility? I'm not hearing your voice.*

Why didn't I just quit? I thought about that many times over those months. But when I first accepted the job, it was clear to me that this was the door God had opened. Whatever was going to happen, He would allow—not necessarily cause, but allow, and there was a purpose to that somehow. When God places you in a position, when He opens the door and says, *This is it—walk through*, only He can tell you it's time to walk out again. Certainly I could have left at any point during that miserable year. As much as I wanted to, something inside was stopping me. God hadn't yet told me it was time to go. I can't walk out of a door that He's opened until He says, *Now we're moving*.

I worked to the best of my ability. I acted with integrity. And I kept praying: *Lord, I need you to come right now and do something with me, because this is what I'm feeling. Here's where I'm at, and I need you to bring me somewhere within myself that I can't get to on my own. I don't have what it takes to forgive.*

Finally, He closed that door. The pieces came together. I saw in my mind's eye, more and more clearly, that I was coming to the end of what I needed to accomplish in that place. The company itself was changing. And I ended up resigning. It was a total miracle from where I stood. I actually felt like I had been promoted.

So what were the greater lessons?

First, you never quite master once and for all the hard task of forgiveness. You never get to a point where you have arrived. You'll slip backward and start all over again, and you always must stay on your knees and ask for God's help.

The second lesson: Thinking back, had I left my job

early on in protest and anger, I would have missed the greater purpose. In fact, the greater purpose was something I don't know yet to this day. A year or two in the future, I may be able to say, "Aha, now I understand. That's what that was all about! Here's what was worked out in my heart and in my soul, in my character and in my maturity. And here's how I have grown and been strengthened because I went through that time."

Third, sometimes you forgive in the dark, in a sense. You may never have an answer or an explanation that will truly satisfy you. Forgiveness is not about understanding why those people did a rotten thing. It's about your willingness to choose to lay it down. That's the Spirit of God at work in us on something that we humans don't possess in and of ourselves.

Don't Wait for an Apology
That May Never Come

Do you need a confession or an apology? That's another human instinct. We want the other guy to fess up. Admit he acted badly. Acknowledge the error of his ways and maybe look sheepish and guilty, and only then can we feel forgiving. Sometimes we'll get that reaction from an offender, but often we won't. And sometimes the offender doesn't even realize his offense, so the only salvation and

hope for moving forward must come from within ourselves. The world isn't about to accommodate our desire to
hear a mea culpa.

One woman talks about a small incident that took place
between herself and a coworker, an incident that she just
can't get beyond in her heart. Sally, whom I mentioned in
an earlier chapter, is twenty-five and works in the billing
department of a health maintenance organization. She's
supporting herself and her year-old son on her own
and living on a tight budget. "This one month I ran into
trouble when our dog, my sweet ten-year-old dog, got
sick. He spent a couple of days at the vet's, and then we
had to have him put to sleep. So that was sad and it was
expensive. I didn't have enough money left over to cover
my utility bill. And I was worried about the service getting
shut off, because that happened once before."

She asked a coworker, Janice, for a loan of $60. "This
was just until our next payday. I have never borrowed
money from anybody at work, in any job I've had, ever. I
sometimes ask my mother to advance me a little, but that's
all, and I always pay it right back. But I felt okay about
asking Janice, because we were friends. We've worked
together for three years. We sit about five feet apart and
we talk all the time and go out for lunch. So I asked her."

Her coworker said, sure, she'd stop at her bank on her
break and take out the cash. "After lunch, Janice came over
to me with the money and a note she had typed up. It said I

owed her this money and I was to sign it. Plus, the amount was for $63. She said she was charging me interest, but only 5 percent, so she was giving me a good deal, because I'd probably have to pay at least 10 percent anywhere else."

Sally was deeply humiliated. She signed the note, stopped by her mother's house that evening, borrowed $63 from her, and repaid Janice the next day. And she can't forgive her. "Janice doesn't seem to think she did anything wrong. Maybe she didn't; I don't even know anymore. Maybe this is just a lesson for me to avoid mixing money and friends. But couldn't she tell that this was so embarrassing to me? It hurt my feelings. That note made it sound like maybe I couldn't be trusted. Plus, what's this cheesy stuff about charging me interest? What kind of a friend does that? I just can't look at her or talk to her anymore, and she's noticed there's a change. I'm waiting for her to apologize."

The apology never came.

That's when laying it down is so hard. That's when forgiveness becomes more than an abstract notion and is felt in the marrow of your bones. Someone's done a hurtful thing, and you have the right to be upset, to cut her off even, and in a worst-case scenario to be vindictive. But what is it getting you? Unless there's the presence of God, I believe, you don't reach the place of understanding. The only person hurt by the anger and resentment and lack of forgiveness that we carry is you.

Especially when the two of you coexist in a small space for eight or more hours a day, you'd better strive to forgive even if you won't forget. Otherwise you are truly creating a toxic atmosphere for yourself, maybe twisting your words and actions into shapes that don't feel good at all. Sally says: "I have been putting on this kind of phony politeness with Janice. It's a strain to keep that up." She was coming up with a new strategy. "I don't know if I can do this and have it come out sounding right, but maybe I can tell her that I'm not blaming her or anything, but that note hurt my feelings. I'm thinking of trying that to clear the air."

Forgive and Hold Accountable

Being a forgiving person yourself doesn't mean that the other guy is off the hook. Your forgiveness does not necessarily exempt him from responsibility, and in many situations it's appropriate to hold that individual accountable and to expect a different behavior.

This is tougher than it sounds, because when you're offended, angry, hurt, or puzzled by someone's actions, you'd just as soon have the whole matter disappear. You don't want to think about it anymore. Maybe there's a head-in-the-sand kind of reaction: "Well, it wasn't so bad what he did. I'm probably making a mountain out of a molehill. I'll forgive him." Or we make excuses: "He's not really responsible because he didn't have the whole story." Or we can condone and look the other way: "That was a one-time thing and it won't happen again; I can write it off." Or we grit our teeth and soldier on.

Start from the place of releasing the emotion. Stop the interior churning. Without laying it down, you can't really analyze or decide on a good course of action. Lack of forgiveness can bind you and hold you prisoner to a situation. Besides, two weeks or six months down the road, you'll respond to a similar situation that pops up in a similar way—in hurt or fury or whatever the emotion you did not release back then. And I believe that when you do start from that place of releasing yourself, you also free your offender to take responsibility.

Here's an example.

Max, whom I've mentioned before, works in the ad department of a pharmaceutical company, and he supervises three subordinates. One young man, James, had been on the job for six months and was generally turning in an outstanding performance. He was also acting in some ways that were infuriating his boss. Max says: "It came to my attention that James was schmoozing with Bill, my boss. James had actually gone to Bill and suggested they have lunch, which they did. Then I found out that James was e-mailing my boss about certain stuff, asking for his feedback, promoting some ideas. I found this out because my boss let drop a couple of times that he'd heard from James about this or that, the guy had some bright ideas, etcetera.

"This was starting to give me heartburn. I was getting totally pissed at this kid. I don't have a problem with one of my staff talking to the big boss, but just out of professional courtesy at the basic level, I ought to know about it. I should give an okay on that. And this was stirring up a whole can of worms because Bill is a guy who relishes any chance to play people off against each other. So he's loving kind of dangling this in front of me, that's he's got an in with my staff and he's hearing stuff. Meanwhile, James is not letting on to me about any of this going on.

"I wanted to fire the guy. Or wring his neck. I was especially offended because I hired him, I brought him along, I gave him the opportunities. This is how he was repaying me. Well, I was starting to act out, as they say, on these very negative feelings I was harboring. In fact, and I'm ashamed to admit this, at one point I intentionally did not pass on to James a piece of information he needed to carry through on one assignment. Talk about shooting yourself in the foot! That's when I pulled myself up short and tried to get objective."

The first thing he realized, Max said, was that James was an excellent salesman, "exactly the kind of talent you want to hold on to in an outfit like this. He was instrumental in making my whole department look good. So I needed to let go of the negativity and see how or if I could bring him in line. I had been after retribution. I wanted to punish the guy by firing him or fouling him up. I decided to go after rehabilitation instead."

He figured out how he could address the issue without being negative or hostile. Max took his subordinate out for a lunch, "and we had a little dialogue on the effect of his actions and then what we needed to do to correct some things. My message to James was something like this: 'I don't mind you talking to Bill—I'm not out to block your access to anybody—but it's not the best professional behavior to do end runs around me. And I need to be in the loop, so if there's any news going back and forth between you and my higher-ups, I need to know that in order to do my job properly.'

"Then I took it a step further and had a word with Bill. I said I appreciated the fact that he valued James, and so forth, but I wanted to make sure we were all on the same page and nobody was getting confused. And maybe it was confusing James and not so good for the business that he, Bill, was going around me. And it also kind of stunted my ability to be able to manage my team."

This all worked like a charm, Max reports. "I think I got all of us back on a better track. We understand each other. It's better for me and it's better for the business. And now I harbor peaceable feelings toward the kid."

Forgiveness is letting go of the offense but not necessarily remaining in a position where you will continue to be offended.

Forgive Yourself Too

He who is without sin, throw the first stone, scripture says. One of my sins is impatience. That impatience produces a lot of drama in my life. It leads to a lot of need for self-forgiveness, which is something I have a tough time with. I have many, many times thought, *I should have known better* or *Oh boy, I did that again—what's wrong with me?* or *Now I've really gone too far*. It leads to asking for a lot of forgiveness as well. I am an analyzer, so I do a lot of mental churning and a lot of picking over the bones of my mistakes.

Forgiving myself is hard because, as we all do, I sometimes forget that God is not like me. I am human and He is not, though He understands what it's like to be human. When I've acted poorly and regretted it, I tend to think, *You know what? If I were God, I wouldn't forgive me for the fifteenth time today*. So it takes me a while to get past it, into the truer thought: *Thank God, He doesn't think the way I do*. God will forgive when we ask.

I believe that when you're able to pardon yourself, it's easier for you to confront your failings and do something about them. It's the actions and people we don't forgive that we have difficulty talking about or being around. No one can then benefit from the experience, because we're still caught in it, really.

I've worked with many people who don't want to fail. They have a need to be perfect, never to hear "This didn't go so well" or "That wasn't right." To them, failing is a huge offense. But unless you take some flops and make some mistakes, you're not leaving yourself open to success. If you're always doing everything right, where is there to go?

Life just isn't a series of successes. Failure is part of the journey.

I think about the times I've fallen flat on my face, on issues or topics or my ability to get work accomplished. In the long run, those have been the greatest moments of growth for me personally and professionally. You learn something. And you take what you learned with you to the next job or to the next issue or assignment.

As I said, impatience is the issue I struggle with most. That's where I most consistently fail, though a little less often today than ten years ago. It is most visible in how I communicate. I may be impatient in a particular situation, but the way I talk about it can come out sounding like a personal attack. I make that individual feel undervalued or belittled. Then, I have a double problem. I've let the impatience rise up and I have disrupted the working relationship between me and a coworker I need to rely on.

In one position, someone on a team I managed had a problem getting his expense report done. I had a call from the finance department that he hadn't submitted his expenses in months and he just wasn't keeping up with the paperwork. This was a young man I'd mentored and coached, and I was very disappointed. No, I was livid. I called him into my office to discuss the situation, telling myself beforehand that I would be patient and not lose it. I gave myself a talking-to: *Okay, no matter what happens here, I'm going to keep it together. I will not show that I am as offended and upset as I am, and we're going to deal calmly and rationally with the situation.*

The conversation began. I explained that the finance department had made me aware that he hadn't completed expense reports in six months, which was against company policy, and I needed to know what was going on.

His response: "I'm really busy. I just haven't gotten around to it."

I let him have it. As I looked at him in not the nicest way, I said something like this: "Excuse me! I get my stuff done on time—I'm beyond swamped—and you're telling me you haven't gotten around to it? Guess what. You make the time. Today. If that takes you until midnight, then you don't leave before midnight. I'm not playing around with this. It's against company policy for you to not have this done. There is no choice here."

Boom. Boom. Boom.

When the conversation was over and he had left my office, I felt terrible. This young man's arrogance had thrown me off guard, but the reality was that whatever was going on at the other end of the table did not give me the right to act inappropriately. I had lost my patience. It didn't matter that I was justified, and it didn't matter that another supervisor might have reacted in a similar fashion. We could have had a better dialogue, and it was my duty to initiate it.

I had to forgive myself for losing it. And then I had to see what I could take away from that awful experience. Since then, for one thing, I've made it clear to people I interview that managing the affairs entrusted to them is vital, particularly if they involve company policy. If there's a difficulty with that, I tell them, we'll have a conversation about it once. If there's a need for a second conversation, they may find themselves off the team.

Mistakes are almost always learning experiences.

Self-forgiveness might be even harder when the offense turns not on a personality flaw, which I might call my impatience, but after a dishonest behavior, as we see in Ellen's story.

Ellen works in a small auction gallery. She describes an incident that happened a year earlier: "I was told to send a letter to a client who was consigning to us a work she owned and was interested in selling. This is a routine practice. The letter provides the client with certain information she needs before making a decision. In this case, I forgot about sending the letter. The client called the gallery owner and said she hadn't heard from us, and the owner asked me what had happened.

"And I lied. I said I'd done the letter on time, it had gone out, and maybe it didn't reach the client or she had misplaced it. That afternoon when the owner was out of the office, I typed up the letter, dating it with the time it was supposedly mailed, made a copy as we always did, and destroyed the original. I showed the copy to my boss, as proof that the thing had been done. I suggested I re-send it to the client, and he said, 'Well, okay.'

"I felt lower than low. I tried to think through all the consequences of my lie, and they were not huge in any business sense. The client got the report, and the worst upshot was that because of the timing, her item couldn't make our current catalogue and she'd be put in a future sale. She was all right with that. The boss said nothing further. But I did what I did just to cover my tail and not look incompetent."

Ellen says she could not get past it in her own mind for a long time. "I came up with explanations. I was desperate to hold on to that job, and I was having money pressures. I'd messed up on something else earlier, and I thought maybe this one would get me booted out, so I took a fairly harmless expediency for the sake of my immediate situation. But the explanations didn't work for me. I felt what I did about that letter showed a lack of character."

Eventually, she says, "I got sick and tired of my own

thoughts, the sound of my own voice. I started to concentrate on the notion of forgiveness, which to me has a biblical connotation, and that's not one that feels entirely natural. Nevertheless, that's what I needed in order to move forward. I told myself that what I had done was shabby, but I wasn't entirely a shabby person. I had to get over that incident—and, really, get over myself. Continuing to beat yourself up over something you did wrong is, in an odd way, attaching a whole lot of importance to yourself in the big scheme of things. It's almost like the negative expression of vainglory.

"And, of course, I resolved not to come out with any more little lies."

Life circumstances can sometimes gang up on us. Family stress, financial or health problems—all kinds of pressures might come together to create weak moments that lead to bad decisions. As humans, we are weak. We screw up; we don't always get it right. Know that God forgives, I believe, and self-forgiveness can follow.

Release Bitterness

Lack of forgiveness leads to bitterness. When you don't release bitterness, it seeps out. Bitterness may be the final, under-the-surface dregs of a situation that calls for understanding and forgiveness.

A friend told me this story. It doesn't have to do with careers, but it has much to do with the principle of forgiveness.

Some years ago, Alice was divorced, and if anyone had reason to hold on to bitterness, it was Alice. She was working two jobs, putting her husband through medical school, and paying all the bills when he announced one day that he'd found someone else. This was a woman also on the way to becoming a doctor, they were in love, and would Alice please move out.

She says: "That was an ugly thing, but a big lesson in forgiveness. I don't talk about that experience a lot, because I dislike pointing to someone else's sin, if you will, or going into chapter and verse about what this person did.

"But the interesting part is, over the years since then, most people I've dated or been in a relationship with have never guessed that I was divorced. One man I've been seeing recently, when I mentioned that I had been married, said, 'Funny, I'd never guess that. You don't act like it. Most divorced people have an edge about them when it comes to relationships. They've got this wall up, a hard core. You're not like that.' I thought that was very telling.

"I forgave my ex-husband. It took a lot of prayer. Going through that awful divorce, what bothered me a lot was that I had made my vows for the rest of my life, and clearly, I wasn't responsible for my husband's behavior and actions. I knew that I was forgiven, because I wasn't involved in the breaking of the vows. But I remember praying so hard, and saying, *God, I do not want to be bitter. I do not want to be a male-basher. We were made for relationships, for love and intimacy, and if I remain angry and vengeful, I remove myself from love and intimacy.* I had that prayer over and over. I remember just knowing in my spirit that the key was to forgive.

"And in time I was released to be free from any of the negative feelings I could have kept inside me. I have friends who've been divorced, and boy, can you tell. It just creeps out in conversation, some of that negativity."

I think she's right. I see it at work so often. I have interviewed or worked with people who are bitter career-wise. Someone's dealt with them badly. Someone's been unfair to them. They have a permanent chip on their shoulder, and what they are capable of doing is completely clouded by that attitude. What's behind the attitude is the hurt, the pain, the disappointment, and the lack of forgiveness they maintain for the person or people who once offended them. People are unaware of carrying that burden, but they do, and it shows.

In conversations about work situations, in interviews, it comes out in guardedness, sometimes a hint of paranoia: *People in the past have done me wrong; it's going to happen again.* Perhaps it's revealed in a sarcastic response or an inappropriate smile or sneer. Perhaps it shows up as a combative stance: *Nobody's going to get the better of me again*. Sometimes, it materializes as a faint aura of sadness, uncertainty, and insecurity.

*O*NE MORE STORY, about the power of bitterness and the greater power that comes with laying it down and forgiving:

Manny works as a porter in a high-rise co-op building. He's been in the job for ten years. Two years ago he was promoted to elevator operator in the same building. Manny explains: "There's the service elevator and the passenger elevator. They're both run by the guys, not automatic. Getting bumped up to passenger elevator operator was kind of a good deal. It's got a little more class to it, you could say. You wear a nice uniform with a tie and your good shoes. There was also some more money in the job and you got first pick on what shifts you wanted."

He had been in the new job for a month or so when the building manager told Manny he was demoting him. There'd been complaints from some tenants; maybe Manny wasn't right for the spot. "I'm a friendly character," Manny says, "and I figured what went wrong was that some of the tenants didn't like me talking to them so much. In fact, I know that's what it was and I know who was doing the complaining. There are a few people in the building, not a lot, that give you that look, like you're not one of them—*You stay over there in your place, pal.*"

So he was back to being a porter, "which is hauling out the trash, mopping the floors, repairing washers." He was hurt and disgusted, and then angry. He tried to start a petition among the tenants to have himself reinstated, but that didn't get off the ground. Manny goes on: "I was walking around in a bad way. This thing affected my personality. I couldn't be friendly. I wasn't even smiling at anybody. This was not a good way to live—I knew that. One day I'm looking through the Bible, and I come to something about the sin of an unforgiving heart and a bitter spirit. No root of bitterness should spring up and cause trouble, it said.

"That was my problem. A bitter spirit was causing trouble for me. I had to get rid of that."

He has a pretty decent job and a wonderful life, Manny says. "I've got a million friends and eight brothers and sisters. I buy two bunches of flowers every Friday, and I bring one to my mom and I put the other one up on my table in my apartment. I love to cook. I love to go to parties. I love to ride my bike through the park. You can't love your life when you've got an unforgiving heart and a bitter spirit."

Maybe what's tough about living out the principle of forgiveness comes down to ego. That's the fight between the spirit of God within you and your own nature. Our ego convinces us that we're better than we think and more important than we are. Our ego persuades us that we know best.

Faith in God tells us something else: Humans make mistakes and need to be forgiven.

Here is how to live
THE PRINCIPLE OF FORGIVENESS:

- Let go and let God: lay down your rights.

- Look for the greater purpose.

- Don't wait for an apology that may never come.

- Forgive and hold accountable.

- Forgive yourself too.

- Release bitterness.

SIX

Stewardship

Using Well the Gifts Bestowed

A STEWARD, says the dictionary, is a person morally responsible for the careful use of money, time, talents, or other resources. To me, that imperative plays out in two arenas: in a career and in a life.

What are your workdays all about? Whether you're a doorman or a doctor, an administrative assistant or a vice president, you have a defined role to fill. It might be the hours you're expected to work, the supplies you've been entrusted with, or the people you're managing. Are you fully engaged and fully responsible?

What is your life all about? What is your calling? Have you put in the time, effort, and prayer to figure out how you're wired and what you're going to do about that? And is your life all about the job, or have you struck a balance between work and everything else?

Being a good steward in both these senses is a challenge for most of us. There are a number of reasons. Once you are on a career path, for one thing, moving along it can claim all your energy and attention. Maybe everyone around you is putting in fifteen-hour days, and you figure you'd better do the same if you want to get ahead. Who has the luxury to worry about creating a balanced life?

At the other extreme, there's often not a great deal of loyalty in the modern business world between the company and the people who work for it. As I talked about at the beginning of this book, a common attitude among employees is this: *They're not really looking out for me, so I don't have to look out for them.*

Then there's the midlife career crisis, when a career path that was rewarding and appropriate no longer seems right. Or it's not enough. You sense that you're not being a very good steward of your talents. But what is next? In fact, you don't have to be middle-aged to start down that line of self-questioning. You wonder: *What am I doing with the gifts that God has bestowed on me? Am I in the right job? Am I putting to full use what I have been given, or do I still have skills and strengths that are just lying dormant inside? Have I reached a point in my job where I'm phoning it in—I can do this with my eyes closed, but shouldn't I be stretching myself?*

Living this principle of stewardship includes both the small actions that crop up in the workplace and the big, "What's it all about?" picture of a lifetime. Here are some thoughts about what it means to be responsible for the careful use of money, time, talents, and other resources.

Be Responsible for the People You Lead

When you manage other people, part of your job is keeping track of how they're doing their jobs.

Sometimes that's facing the reality that an individual you're supervising isn't getting the work done. That's always a hard place. I talked earlier about having the tough conversation, when it's right to do so.

It's a leader's responsibility to be clear and informative to the people around him or her, whatever that takes. I've noticed that many individuals are in leadership roles because they have a title, not because they're truly leading anyone. Many often don't want to have the tougher conversations with their team. But stewardship is thinking: *This person is under my charge for forty hours a week. Am I going to make her life richer and more productive as a result of having worked with me, or not? Is she going to grow? And if she's not doing the job, what's the right step for me and for the company?*

To help me make those decisions, I use the following criteria: Does this person execute? Is she successful in building necessary relationships here? When I start seeing that after a couple of attempts, someone just isn't getting it, I have a conversation and ask what's going on, relying solely on facts supported by examples: "You were given this assignment with this deadline. It wasn't done on time; it wasn't done in final form. Is there an explanation?" There's always a need to operate in wisdom, looking at all surrounding issues. Some aspects of a work environment you can't totally control, after all, and you can't expect the people who work for you to control them either.

If the problems continue over the next month or two, we have another dialogue. If we get nowhere over time, I will make the difficult decision to let the person go.

We're stewards, too, of the tools we're handed for getting our jobs done. I've always said to my team members that we don't own the department we're in and we don't own the things we've been given authority over; they belong to the company. They are loaned to us as part of this job for a purpose for this company—down to the pen that I'm using: It's not mine; it belongs to someone else. And our job is to leave what we were entrusted with somehow better than how we found it.

For some people, that concept is a stretch. I have worked with individuals who believe that because the company employs them, they're owed something. Or that what nobody sees doesn't matter. Or *This is a rich outfit. I'm not a rich person; I can take a few liberties.*

A manager in one marketing department of a large entertainment company confronted that attitude in one of his employees. Walter says: "This young guy was enjoying doing his own thing a little too much. For instance, we're pretty casual about lunchtime around the office. I don't care if somebody wants to go out at eleven in the morning or two in the afternoon, but it's company policy that lunch hour is that—an hour. And Gordon, my worker, was abusing that. He'd be gone for a couple of hours sometimes. I had to talk to him about it, and he pulled himself back in line."

Gordon behaved in other ways that were even more troubling to his boss. "In this business, you can call manufacturers or suppliers and ask for complimentary copies of their products, as a professional courtesy. Nothing high end, but small handheld electronic games, things of that nature. These products are requested and looked at for various business purposes.

"So, one day I'm passing by Gordon's desk and I hear him on the phone asking to have this particular gadget shipped to his attention. A couple of weeks later, I overhear a similar call. So I got my antenna up and started keeping a closer eye on Gordon. He got in a lot of packages all the time, which didn't make sense for his assignments, as far as I could see. After he left the office one evening, I went over to his desk and opened the bottom drawer, and this large drawer is filled with games, CDs, videos, all in their original packages. A couple of days after that, I watch him loading up a shopping bag with all this loot and heading out. I put two and two together and figured he was hawking this stuff somewhere."

Walter called Gordon in for a talk, and to his amazement, his assistant readily admitted that he was selling the products at half retail price in a shop he knew, and he didn't see anything too wrong with that. "This guy felt that he wasn't getting paid much, he deserved a higher salary, and this little side business he had going was his way of getting some bucks the company owed him. Plus, he told me other people in the place took things all the time, like packets of printer paper. I told him that's stealing and that wasn't going to happen on my watch, and he was fired."

Walter didn't believe his talk with Gordon, or even his firing of Gordon, was going to make much difference to the young man. "There's a saying that the teacher comes when the student is ready. This kid wasn't ready to be a student who could learn something from me about the right and the wrong way to work for a company. He wasn't listening."

I think Walter's correct about that. Gordon was using his position not for the benefit of the people who gave it to him but for his own enrichment. He didn't hear that, however. The way we do what we're asked to do is our signature, and how we sign things we do comes from our heart's motivation. That's where our relationship with God, and our spiritual maturity plays a key role.

Two other thoughts about this matter of leading by the principle of stewardship:

First, godly stewardships means acting for the good of the company, not just for yourself or for your team. When people start getting into organizational politics, and I see this all the time, decisions are made not on the basis of whether a direction is for the overall betterment of the company but whether they can help promote a particular individual or a particular agenda that is not necessarily good overall. To me, that's not proper stewardship. There are decisions I've made in my positions that maybe were not the best for me—because they meant more work, for one thing—but were in the best interests of the organization. And those are the decisions I was hired to make.

Second, in the ideal demonstration of stewardship, you return the department, the job, whatever it is, in even better shape than you found it. That's illustrated by the biblical parable of the talents: Two servants are given ten talents each. The master goes away. After a period of time, he returns, and he hears from one servant, "You gave me ten talents. I buried them, and here they are back, just as they were." The other servant, however, has doubled his talents, and he finds God's favor. He was given little, and because he did something with the little, he will be given much more. I have found that whether the much more comes immediately or later, somewhere else, or in the same place, "the more" will come.

Don't Give Your Life to the Job

Jesus said to render to Caesar what is Caesar's and to God what is God's. In the context of work, that means give to the office what it deserves and to the rest of your life what it deserves. It also means recognizing your workaholic ways and whether they are preventing you from developing a balanced and spiritual life. A simple thing I've discovered is that whatever controls and dominates you, that is your god. If what controls and dominates you is career ambition, career success, and the material prizes that come with it, you've made that your life purpose. And chances are, your life is probably not very balanced.

Workaholic ways are something I know a lot about. I've been there and back—and learned a few things. For example, it's easy to be a workaholic when you don't really want to think about what else is missing in your life. Let me tell you my story.

Throughout my twenties and most of my thirties, I was focused with laserlike intensity on what I had to get under my professional belt if I was going to be a high-level executive, running a global department, by age forty. I was after managerial experience, regional experience, international experience. All these qualifications I felt I needed as part of my long-term strategy.

During those years, I usually traveled twenty-seven days out of the month. That's all I did. If I was sick, I'd just medicate on the road and keep going. The truth of the matter is, when I look back, all that focus not only was serving my career but it also enabled me to avoid issues I didn't really want to deal with. I didn't want to examine what it meant that I was not married yet. And that I didn't have family where I lived or that I kept moving around on my own from place to place. I didn't want to ask myself why I was missing siblings' birthdays and my parents' anniversaries and still not finding complete joy out of my career.

I didn't want to acknowledge that sometimes I was lonely, so it was all too easy to bury myself in my work. My social life was mainly with people I met through my job or my colleagues in the office. That was no stretch; you have a point of reference, a common context, and there's no need for the getting-to-know-you dance. So while my career was going relatively well—as it should have, since I was dedicating twenty-four hours a day to it—there was no balance. Work was the majority of what I thought about and did.

Eventually, I got the message: That wasn't a great way to live. But it took some drama for the message to get through.

At one point, I worked myself into the ground so badly that I developed walking pneumonia. The doctor said, "Either I have you hospitalized or you get somebody to come care for you at home. Those are your options before you leave this office." My mom flew up. It was my second day in bed that it hit me, just how deathly ill I was. I was home from work for three weeks.

A week or so into this, as she was leaving some juice by my bed, my mom looked at me and said, "You know, right about now you might want to ask yourself what God is trying to say to you. You've clearly been stopped in your tracks."

Still, I didn't really get it. I didn't learn the whole lesson then.

On another occasion, I flew into a city to attend some meetings, after I'd been on the road for two weeks. Business trips had become like clockwork for me: get off the plane, retrieve my bags, go to the rental car desk, pick up a car. I pulled out of the parking lot of the airport, drove off down the road, and suddenly had a full-blown panic attack. I had no idea where I was or where I was supposed to be going. I freaked out.

I pulled off onto the side of the road and sat there, and I can't begin to describe the sheer terror that hit me. *Where am I?* The obvious steps—get out my maps, look at my itinerary—didn't occur to me. I'd lost my memory and my mind, and I just sat there.

Next thing I knew, there were lights behind me, a knock on my window, and a police officer asking, "Ma'am, are you all right?" I said, "I don't know where I am." He asked again, "Are you all right?" And I said, "No, I'm really exhausted and I got confused."

He told me where I was, and then, thank God, it came back to me what I was doing there. I was able to tell him why I was there, this was where I was going, this was the place I had to drive to. I needed to convince the officer that I was okay to go. "All right," he said, "but you need to get some rest."

I drove off thinking, *No, I need to get a life—that's what I need to do.*

Other times I'd wake up in the middle of the night, in a hotel room, and wonder what city I was in. And have to concentrate hard in order to get my bearings again. Any of this sound familiar?

It reached a point where I would show up at church back in my town and feel out of the loop there as well. I wasn't building a sense of community where I was living. I wasn't living; I was existing—and just for the benefit of the people who were paying me. I wasn't even enjoying the fruits of my labor or what I was accomplishing.

Finally, my thoughts were: *It is God who has brought me this far. And do I have the kind of life that honors His purpose and the path He has set me on? I have a career, but what else have I built?* That's when I began to understand the lack of balance to my days, and to look hard at what I was missing.

It took not one but a couple of walking-pneumonia episodes, a little touch of amnesia from time to time, and reaching my mid-thirties to get there. But it made a big difference in how I pursued my career from then on. When interviewing for a new position now, I'll draw my line in the sand. It sounds something like this: "I visit my parents for their birthdays and on the holidays. Occasionally I take time off to go on mission trips with my church. I leave work right at five on Tuesdays, because I have a church service that evening. Is that going to be okay here? If it's not, we should end this interview now. I won't be good for you and you won't be good for me." I say it all up front, because I don't want to be hired with the expectation that I will be an indentured servant.

On the job, I delegate more now. I go to only the "must attend" business events. I book my vacation way ahead of time and let everyone know I'm not changing it for a last-minute meeting. It must be a life-or-death issue in order for me to reschedule, because if I'm all that important, I should be somewhere else making a whole lot more money.

When you establish a decent balance between work life and personal life, it has a ripple effect. If I'm at work at six in the morning and still there at eight at night, I'm setting a standard for the people around me, the people I'm accountable to, and it's not the best standard. I'm sending out a message that the job tops all, and if your personal life or your family suffers, too bad. When I strive for balance, others feel more comfortable coming to me and saying, "My mom's in town, and I'd like to leave early on Friday."

Balance comes from having your priorities set. It's saying: *What do I need to accomplish today to meet the priorities of my life as I understand them?* For me, that is God, spouse, family, work, personal pleasures, and rewards.

Prioritizing like this is not as easy as it sounds and may not come so naturally, not after a lifetime of doing everything the other way around. Every now and then, I have to remind myself to analyze and measure my workweek and be careful what I commit to.

If you, too, recognize that your workaholic ways have been dominating your life, maybe it's time to think more carefully about your stewardship over your life. You've been given X number of years on this earth. What are you doing with them? Are you accomplishing what God has sent you here to accomplish? Have you bothered to find out what that is, or have you been too busy working? Find out. Because one day, just like the man with the talents, you too will be asked what you did with yours.

Give Your All to the Job When You're on the Job

Giving your all to work when you're at work is the other side of the coin. When you're there, being a good steward of your work life means being fully there.

All of us are in danger of mentally checking out occasionally. Life bleeds into work. There are days when you've got to call the doctor, something has come up with the kids, there's an issue at home. We're at our desks, but only 75 percent really present. However, when you are consistently not present while you're at work, that's when you get in trouble. It happens most when employees start feeling that their company isn't loyal to them, and so they don't owe the company anything. And that's not true. There's the issue of stewardship: If I'm hired to do my job to the best of my ability, that's my assignment, regardless of my thoughts about the company's loyalty to me.

I've been through periods like that. There's been a new policy, a new boss, a shift in the organization, something that leads me to put in the hours but not the commitment. I'm skimping. I've had to call myself to task on that—meet my responsibilities with full attention while thinking over my options.

Maybe the company is wrong. But two wrongs don't make a right.

A woman who works for a major financial organization describes that situation. "I was heading up the employee assistance program," says Claire, "and over ten years, under my direction, the department had moved into a number of new areas. We started out doing basic health and mental health issues. We broadened the service to provide alcohol counseling, stress management, retirement counseling, executive coaching, family–work life balance counseling—very exciting and worthwhile efforts. My team and I met with over a thousand people a year.

"Then the change. Essentially, my department was being downsized or maybe eventually would be abolished, though nobody said that in those words. Some of the services we provided were now being outsourced, obviously for cost-cutting purposes, and I had to let some of my department staff go. A lot of what we'd been doing became less important or just didn't happen. Our efforts weren't funded or weren't given the level of attention needed to succeed.

"And that, of course, led to *Well, Claire, you're not doing such a good job; you're not being successful*. I couldn't be successful because I was no longer getting the backing I needed. There was no way I could win."

Claire fell into a the-hell-with-them attitude about her job. "I started thinking, *Okay, fine. I don't intend to retire from this place in twenty years. They're paying me to show up, and I will, but I'm not giving it my all*."

Any organization you work for is entitled to shift the direction its business is going in. Unless your name is on the building, the company can do whatever it wants. So ask yourself the productive questions: *Do I have a conversation with my boss about added resources? Is another assignment possible for me? Can I get better information about what's coming up over the next six months or the next year and how I will fit into those plans?* And sometimes the question is: *Should I remain here, or should I look for another environment?*

Follow a Dream

Maybe it's not even a particular dream but just a strong sense that there's something more—or something else—out there for you. Can you reach for it? And if you don't, what does that say about being a good steward of your life? When you don't give it a shot, whatever it may be, the consequences inevitably creep out in negative ways.

A friend tells this story: Connie leads a busy life, with a full-time job, a husband, and three minor children. She hired a housekeeper who hated being a housekeeper.

Connie says: "I happened to come across this saying from the Gospel of Thomas. 'If you bring forth what is within you, what you bring forth will save you. If you do not bring forth what is within you, what you do not bring forth will destroy you.' I thought, *Oh wow, that says it all about Lisa*, the housekeeper we took on.

"Lisa lives in the neighborhood. She has two daughters, whom her mother babysits. She ran errands for people, did some housekeeping and cleaning for several families, some catering. Lisa's husband is a handyman and carpenter, and he was apparently happy with the status quo. Lisa wanted more. She actually said to me, several times, 'This is not the kind of life I want.'

"It affected her job with us, because I asked her to do things around the house that she felt were beneath her. One day we were having a small confrontation about this over the phone, and she said bluntly, 'I don't want this. There's more for me than housekeeping.' I said that I didn't disagree about that, and she should probably find what that more was and go for it, but I was hiring her for this job now. She started crying. She said, 'My mother doesn't support me, my husband doesn't support me; they just don't understand why I can't be satisfied with what I have.'

"It became an untenable situation. Toward the end of her time with us, she had a negative attitude about almost everything she was asked to do. And this was really just routine light cleaning, some laundry, the typical tasks you expect from a housekeeper. I felt bad for her. I believe she had ambition and drive, and she was surrounded in her life by people who thought there was something wrong with her. I would say she was not bringing forth what was within her, and what she was not bringing forth was destroying her."

If you don't like what you're doing, then find something you do like. Those are easy words to say but hard to live by. For many of us—most of us, really—making money comes first. Feeling satisfaction about how the money arrives is nice if you can get it, but not critical. And options aren't always apparent. But I believe that when you're miserable, God is telling you it's right to reach elsewhere. Otherwise, not only do you stay miserable but you also take it out on the people you work around or work for.

We see that all the time. Walk into certain establishments, request service from someone who's expected to provide it, and you're face-to-face with an obviously unhappy, disgruntled person. As a customer, you think, *Go get a job that you can smile at.* In meetings in corporate life it's clear when someone doesn't want to be there, doesn't want to be doing what he or she is there to do. It always shows. It's no way to live your one God-given life.

The story of Lisa, the housekeeper, ended well, from all appearances. Connie says: "I spoke to her recently. This was about a year after she'd left working for us. In that time, she'd gotten a real estate license and she was actively invested in that business. She was just beaming, and so much happier. She was a changed person. She also told me her marriage had ended. So bringing forth what was within her saved her in one way, but there was a price to pay. Maybe it hadn't been a good marriage all along and she was glad to be out of it; I really don't know. So perhaps it all came together as it was meant to be."

A calling can emerge slowly and point toward some future, still unformed plans.

Edie works as a project manager and profile writer in the legal department of a pharmaceutical company. She entered the company seven years ago right out of college and has moved up several ranks in that time. She's not planning a change of job any time soon but has been thinking a lot about her calling in life.

Edie says: "I began as a literacy volunteer with the Head Start program while I was still in college, and I've been volunteering ever since. When I began, I had no idea what a rewarding experience it would be. Not only was I helping children with their reading skills but also I felt as though they really looked forward to seeing me each week, as I did them. I learned how important it was to have an extra person in their lives who cared and made time for them. They began opening up with a more positive attitude.

"In working with children and adolescents, specifically with girls with adjustment problems and self-esteem issues, I realized the importance of mentoring and the need for teen advocacy programs. And that ultimately led to my desire to work someday in the human services industry. I'm pursuing a master's degree in applied psychology. Eventually, I would like to go after my Ph.D. and work in the human services industry, focusing on mentoring and wellness programs in the community, perhaps serving on a health advocacy committee and ultimately pursuing studies in holistic wellness.

"I believe that each job brings you a step closer to your calling. Even one small step is progression. Work experience as a project manager helped me to get organized and become a better planner in achieving my life goals. My experience as a profile writer in reviewing product liability cases has raised an awareness that there is a health crisis and a need for holistic wellness.

"This is a quote I like: 'Only with the realization that each person has the opportunity to give back can humankind reach its true potential.' "

It boils down to purpose.

One man took a sudden about-face in his life. Eric was working in a bank, at a job that bored him, and one night he went to a play with some friends. It had the unanticipated effect of "jolting me awake," he says. "The play was called *Sailor's Song*, by John Patrick Shanley. Some of the dialogue just hit me strong, and I went back and looked it up, because I wanted to remember the words. This main character, a sailor, says at one point that he'd been all over the world, but he couldn't find any reason for his life. 'A breakthrough cause, something that puts me on the other side, you know, with the people who knew why they're alive.' Without that, he says, 'Then I'm just another guy waiting to die.'

"Whoa! That was me. I decided I'd just been too damn lazy to hunt up a breakthrough cause for myself."

The monotony of his job was exhausting him. Eric says: "You'd think if you're doing something dull all day to make a buck, then you're ready to cut loose in the evening or the weekends. But instead, I was tired—tired not in the sense of not getting enough sleep, but mentally tired. Or spiritually tired. Actually, I was probably sort of depressed. And I'm still a young guy, so I started thinking nothing good could come of this for me in the long run."

He worked with a group of mostly men, and they'd arrived at banking jobs in similar ways. "We were all economics majors in college. We got recruited right after graduation, though a couple of guys were also going for MBAs. I shared space with a fellow named Paul, and I started paying attention to what he was like on the job, and I saw the difference between him and me. He just loved this work. A lot of what he did was brokering deals. One time, he was about to leave for a couple days in Los Angeles to arrange the sale of some airplanes, and he was pumped, just so up and happy. Doing the deal was what made him feel alive."

Eric pulled his about-face. He quit the bank and took a job teaching French in a prep school. "I always liked the academic atmosphere. I studied French all through high school and minored in it in college, and when I started this teaching spot, I took to it like a duck to water. This life is totally different from the bank life. Different hours. Different interactions with people. Different clothes I wear. Way different money, that's for sure. Next year will be my third year at it, and I'm taking a small study group to Paris on break. It's all good."

Strive for Balance

I asked Anthony, a computer programmer, to talk about the concept of living a life in balance—what it means and how you know if you've achieved it. He thought that over for a long time. Then he wrote this reply:

I want to tell you about my father.

He died two years ago, age ninety. He came to the United States when he was about three or four, I think, with his family, from Austria. They settled in New Jersey, and the kids—my dad, his two brothers, and two sisters—pretty much all started working at early ages. He did all kinds of odd jobs. Then he landed a job with the phone company and put himself through college part time, taking a two-year break once when he ran out of money.

So finally with a degree in electrical engineering, he decided to keep on with the phone company, and he stayed there until he retired at age sixty-five. He married my mother, they had my two sisters and me, and I do not think he ever missed a day's work in forty years. He was a tough old bird, never got sick, or ignored it if he did. But he also had that indomitable work ethic.

But here's where the idea of balance comes in.

He and my mom were completely different as far

184

as interests go. She was kind of artistic, actually kind of arty. Liked the theater and going to museums. Dad was athletic and loved all sports, and physical activity generally. He told me a story once, when he was an old man and Mom had already passed away. They had a four-day honeymoon in Bermuda when they got married. He took his golf clubs and, very big deal, he bought a left-handed set of clubs for her. She was a lefty. He had a vision of them golfing together. They got there and she wanted no part of it. The clubs never left the bag.

So on the morning before they were to go home, he went out on the course. There was nobody around. He teed off and started walking after his ball. Then he came upon a banana tree, he said, with ripe bananas on it, and he sat down under the tree and slowly ate a banana. He stayed there for a long time, and then he picked up his clubs and walked back to the hotel.

There is something so poignant to me about that scene. Now, I'm imagining this, of course, but I picture him sizing things up in his mind. I'm thinking maybe he knew what he was in for, and it wasn't going to be so easy. Maybe he was going to be on his own in some ways.

Back to the "balance" theme. All his life he was involved in sports. In college, he did running, gymnastics, swimming. In adulthood, he was on the

Tuesday-evening bowling team at work, back when they had those things. He golfed as often as he could. He went fishing. We had a little house, just a summer bungalow out on the island, and he commuted into the city from there during the summers, taking two long subway rides because the railroad was too expensive. When he got home on those summer evenings, he went down to the beach and swam back and forth in the ocean. Sometimes I went with him and watched, and he was a powerful swimmer, way out there in the ocean. He did all those things on his own.

He took care of my grandparents, my mother's folks, who lived with us during the summers. Nobody else knew how to drive a car, so he was always shuttling people around. He took care of that bungalow. He put on a new roof, built a room out back, rewired the place. They never had much money, but he put all three of us through college.

I don't remember me or my sisters or anybody ever thanking him for all that, to our shame. But he never acted like he expected any thanks.

He was an amateur inventor of anything to do with electronics. After he retired, he got involved with a hospital for children with chronic diseases, and he made for them a series of dolls with simulated heartbeats. These were apparently soothing to the sick babies, according to research he studied. He did all this in his basement workshop. He spent hours down there while my mom was off somewhere else.

All and all, I think my parents had a strong and good marriage. It must have been, since it thrived for sixty-one years. And I think he was a happy man, or at least a man at peace with himself. He had his professional career, his family loves and responsibilities, his athletic life, his hobbies, and his good works. All things in balance.

Be the steward of
YOUR WORK AND YOUR LIFE:

- Be responsible for the people you lead.

- Don't give your life to the job.

- Give your all to the job when you're on the job.

- Follow a dream.

- Strive for balance.

SEVEN

Legacy

Setting a Course for Those Who Follow

$\mathscr{A}$T A MEETING of business professionals, I suggested that we discuss the idea of legacies and what each of us hoped ours would be. One man spoke up: "Well, I'm not lofty enough to assume that I'm going to leave a legacy." I think he thought he was responding with humility.

Like it or not, plan for it or not, believe in it or not, we all leave a legacy from our working days and our lives. We leave a message of who we were, what we stood for, and how we went about our jobs. The people we worked with will remember, our children will remember from the stories we share and the way they see us prioritize work and family life and everyone we touch along the way. When you are in a role that enables you to shape the life of another human being, be it your own child or that of a coworker, it's pretty serious and pretty important, and a privilege. It doesn't have much to do with being lofty. In fact, it doesn't necessarily involve holding leadership positions and managing people. We all make a mark.

Over the course of a career, creating a worthwhile legacy happens in two ways. One is through modeling the spiritual principles we've discussed in this book—integrity, forgiveness, faith, humility, stewardship. It's a work in progress, from day one until I walk out the door and turn off the lights for the last time. Not only is God always watching, but so are the people around me. Everyone, everywhere, all the time, and sometimes you won't even know who's really noticing. But unless you're laboring away in solitude on a deserted island, your career or workdays are always playing out before an audience. You are a role model in your behavior—for better or worse. It all feeds into the legacy you create.

Then there are the actions we consciously decide on, such as actively opening doors and extending a hand to those coming up behind you through formal and informal mentoring and other helpful efforts. Maybe you become a voice for people who don't have a voice, or you tell your story in the hopes that others will be enriched by it.

Leaving a legacy is really about being a role model and mentoring and other ways we leave a mark. Having a relationship with God means we are mirroring Him to the world. So the things we say or don't say, the actions we take or don't take, they all tell others who God is, at least in small ways.

Reach Out to Those Who
Are Not Like You

In the workplace, for women and people of color especially, there is still a long road we must travel to be heard
and counted. We all have had feelings and experiences that
may have been unpleasant or unwarranted, because of
gender or culture or age.

I have had occasion in corporate life to be involved in
and lead the developing diversity programs and practices.
My personal experiences as an immigrant, a woman, and a
Hispanic, as I've described them over the previous chapters, have certainly impelled me to be an advocate for the
inclusion of all kinds of people. Everyone should find a
place at the table. It's good for business.

The challenges I have faced in my career both inspired
and educated me. One thing I came to understand: Diversity is something everyone at all levels should encourage.
The white male population is the one that historically has
been running the show. And so yes, the responsibility falls
heavily on that group, I believe, to create a more equitable
work environment. But women and people of color must
also be aware of the need for inclusion and work to promote it in job environments. We don't have the whole picture unless all pieces of the puzzle are represented where
the decisions are being made.

Diversity is not just about ensuring fair employment

practices—seeing that women and minorities are fully represented. In the organizations I've worked for, it also means reaching out to multicultural market segments. If we know that X number of Hispanics and X number of African-Americans use our products, for example, are we advertising in media that they're most likely to look at?

At the personal, one-on-one level, however, there are opportunities to open up wider dialogues and promote understanding. It's often a tricky business. You can never completely know, not really, someone else's life experiences and exactly how they have been shaped by them. That sometimes makes for awkward moments or guarded behavior or a whole lot of political correctness that gets in the way of people talking comfortably to one another and truly connecting.

A woman who works in a large real estate firm hired a new administrative assistant who was of Asian descent. Polly says: "This young woman, Lily, had a very nice résumé and I had no doubt she'd fit right in at our place. She started catching on to the job immediately. I noticed her excellent phone manner. And I was also intrigued by her looks. She's a tiny person, size 2, I'd say. That shiny, sleek black hair. Beautiful dresser. One day I said to her, just because I was curious, 'Lily, are you Korean?' She paused for a couple of beats, and then she said yes, she was, and turned back to her computer.

"Now, I don't know how to explain this exactly, but I

had the awful feeling I'd offended her, just from a look in her eyes. I'd triggered something. I wondered about it all afternoon. Was that a rude question? Was I supposed to have known her background from her last name, which I didn't? Or, and this is kind of terrible, did it sound like I was saying I can't tell the difference between Korean or Japanese or Chinese or whatever, because everybody looks alike?"

A couple of days later Polly invited her assistant out for lunch. "I asked her about her family, and she talked about growing up in Southern California, her father's import business, the extended relatives, and big holiday dinners. I didn't say anything about maybe having offended her. It wasn't necessary. I was genuinely interested in what she had to say, and we had a nice chat. I think we both felt comfortable by the end, and I even told her I was envious of her gorgeous hair!"

Another woman describes her workplace environment as "Them over there and us over here. We have a very mixed staff; there's no hostility. But the minority folks stick together and the nonminority folks stick together when it comes to hanging out; things like leaving work, going on coffee breaks. There's not a lot of intermingling."

More mingling is probably good for all of us. Laws dictate what we can and can't do in many of these business-related issues surrounding diversity. But laws don't shape our hearts. And people of color and from minority backgrounds can have history or baggage others can only guess at. Polly, the woman with the Korean assistant, says: "I remember years ago, back in high school, I had a girl-friend who was Chinese. We went to a diner for Cokes after school one day, and this waiter looked at my friend and made a kind of disgusting racial remark. He thought this was funny; he was laughing. My friend said nothing, but we never went to that place again. I was thinking about that in connection with the Lily thing, that if you've run into a few incidents like that growing up, it probably leaves scar tissue. It makes you suspicious of people's meanings and intentions. And on the other side of the fence, you can't totally understand what it's like to come from that place and what might have triggered their inappropriate behavior."

Meeting people where they are and with empathy will always teach us something. It means tearing down the walls between the spiritual life and the everyday working life. Relationship with God will bring you to the under-standing that there should be no walls.

Personally, I have always made it a practice not to spend all my time with people just like me. I bore myself some-times—my own thoughts, my own way of being. Sitting around in a roomful of other people like me can get doubly boring and exhausting. You need people around you to snap you back into reality and to present you with some-thing new and different.

Be There for Children

A teenage stepson entered my life a few years ago. My daughter was born more recently. So I've come—somewhat later in life, at age forty—to give thought to this matter of children and legacy.

Being a stepparent is a great gift and a delicious treat. I love my stepson, I want him to live a good and successful life, and I hold him in my prayers every day. There are the times I can step in with advice and be heard in a way that maybe his own parents won't be heard. Those are unique opportunities to offer guidance. He says, "Well, yeah, sure, my mom would say that, my dad would say that; that's what parents always say." And I'm in the position of being able to come back and say, "Okay, but I'm starting from a different place, I have no axe to grind here, and still this is what I'm thinking," and so on. That's the nice part, to be relatively free of all that parent–child tension. He and I can be friends.

To me it's a blessing to think that he is fifteen years old now and in fifteen years, he'll be thirty years old and I will have known him since he was twelve. I look forward to an even more robust relationship than the one we have now, adult to adult.

With my new daughter, my hope is that in time I will be able to make that same transition, from being the grown-up who establishes rules and guides and teaches to the supportive friend. Along the way, I'm sure she will benefit from the fact that I've lived an interesting and productive life. I've gained knowledge and experience from the working world that she gets to inherit, in a sense. I picture my little girl coming to me with a problem or a worry, and me saying, "Well, kiddo, let me tell you about some times when people didn't accept me either" or "I was sure I was going to fail, too, but I didn't and here's why." Coming to parenthood at a somewhat advanced age after a couple of decades in the job world means you have useful insights to pass along. But more importantly, the greatest gift we will leave our children is the heritage of praying parents.

There's a saying in scripture: Train a child in the way he should go, and when he is older he will not turn from it.

My daughter and stepson will find their own way to God. It's always personal. Obviously, while she's still a little kid, my daughter will go to the same church we attend, she will participate in the same things we participate in, and we will attempt to instill certain values in her. However, just as I had a time in my life when I said to God, *Here I am,* she will have to do that for herself. Because I walk with God and have a relationship with Him doesn't mean she automatically inherits that. She does, however, inherit the legacy of parents who have a relationship with God, so she sees what that means for our lives both at work and at home.

My prayer for my daughter is: *God, may she know you, and may she know you in an even more powerful way than I*

*do, that she may have more revelation than I have, even faith,
so that the next generation may be even stronger spiritually.*
From there, God will do His part to move her heart.

I wanted to call this section "Be There for Children"
because that notion gets to the heart of how the career life
and the parenting life meet. What does "being there"
mean? It's an old issue by now; reams have been written
on the subject of working moms and stay-at-home moms.
I think of it here, however, in the sense of legacy and what
message we send our children. It has to do with spiritual
purpose and calling, with balance, and with knowing when
you know that you know.

$\mathcal{A}$NN MARIE TALKS about returning to work in
the retailing field after her child was born. "I went back to
my job when she was three months old. There were practical considerations. We were all covered under my health
insurance, so that was a big one. My husband was a self-
employed computer technician. He could set up appoint-
ments partly according to his own schedule, and he stayed
with the baby in the mornings and then he brought her to
our neighbor's for the afternoons.

"It wasn't a piece of cake, of course. But I never had
that feeling you hear about, that as a working mother
you're never either fully here or there—on the job, your
head is back at home, and at home, you're thinking of

the job. Maybe if I had more trouble with child-care arrangements I might have felt differently. But I loved my work, I wanted to be there, and I saw a future in it. And I loved my child and being a mom.

"Not long after I went back, we had a new boss come in. She was not much older than me, tough as nails, divorced, the stereotypical career woman. She was taking the employees out one at a time for breakfast meetings. It came my turn, and I was not looking forward to it. It was not a very relaxed breakfast, but okay. When we were leaving, though, she said something completely unexpected. She had two young children, and they lived in an apartment about thirty blocks uptown from our offices. And she said, 'I never want to work in a place where I couldn't run home on my own two feet if my kids were in trouble or needed me.' I had a new admiration for her. I bet her children knew that they came first. And I thought, *If you keep your priorities straight, things won't go too far off the rails.*"

Ann Marie's child is eighteen today, "and the best kid you'd ever want."

*M*ARA IS A NIGERIAN WOMAN, a physical therapist by training, married to a doctor. She describes herself as "strong type A." She knows that she's called now to leave her profession in order to be an at-home mother to her child.

In an e-mail message to me, Mara said she considers it an honor and a privilege to serve God by raising a new generation of Christians. Someday, she may go back to physical therapy work, "but this is where I'm supposed to be now." She sees her mission and role in the bigger scheme of things, and she witnesses changes in herself as a person, good changes she could not have anticipated.

*E*LEANOR, IN HER LAST MONTH of pregnancy, was urged by a friend to take a tour of a school in their town, for future reference. At the time, she was debating within herself the issue of going back to work versus staying at home, and she talked that over with the school's director. Most of the kids there had mothers who didn't work outside the home, Eleanor figured, and that probably made things easier for everybody. The director said: "I'll tell you something funny about that. I find that the women who go back to their careers have the best systems and the best support for their kids. If a child here is acting up or sick, we can pick up the phone and call the mom, and within thirty minutes there will be someone here to pick that child up. You know where to reach them; they have measures in place. With the stay-at-home moms, we've often got to track them down. They could be at lunch with friends or playing tennis, for example."

That was a unique perspective, Eleanor thought, and it

gave her comfort. "I looked at the skills I use in the corporate arena, and it struck me that a lot of what I've learned and what I'm good at is going to help me in being a mother even if I'm back at the job. Time management, project management, keeping on top of schedules, and balancing competing interests; I have twenty years behind me in picking up those strengths. So it's not going to be all of a sudden, *Wow! How do I learn to do this mom thing?*"

ROSE HAS TWIN SONS, five years old. She quit work when they were born. Rose says: "My mom was always around when I was a kid, and I think that's important. My husband, he's the pied piper. He takes the boys over to the playground on Saturdays, and in ten minutes he's got fifteen other kids tagging after him. I don't have that knack for being playful, I guess you'd say; I'm more of a worrier. But that's okay. We have two happy, lively little boys. I believe in my heart of hearts that I should be home with them and I want to be home with them. I'm at peace in my heart about that."

THAT'S THE COMMON THREAD: peace in the heart. Hearing your calling and knowing your purpose, as it exists right now. Some find it in being a stay-at-home parent; others find it in work outside the home. For me and for many others, it's answering the question *Am I using my skills and talents the way God would have me use them?* When the grown-ups are at peace, so are the children. And as time goes on, they're listening and watching what we do—a silent audience to our example of living with purpose.

I look back at my father.

I saw him put on a uniform every morning and drive a meat delivery truck: sides of beef, sometimes a whole cow. At night, he washed dishes at the pizza place down the street. He moved his way up the ranks at the meatpacking company and went from a blue-collar to a white-collar job as a salesperson in the same organization, with a company car and customers to visit. Now retired, he still works a part-time job in the meatpacking business, a business he's been in for almost forty years. Everybody in South Florida knows him—restaurant owners, supermarket owners, and small bodega owners. Some of them have known him from when he was wearing a uniform with his first name on it, driving the truck and hauling beef, to when he would walk in wearing a suit and tie as a salesperson.

I remember the times that I was hitting a softball or kicking a soccer ball. My father would be in the stands, wearing a dress shirt and tie, sometimes the only father around at 5:30 PM on a work night. He rarely missed a game. It wasn't until I was in the workplace and watched so many of my male colleagues work late hours that I real-

ized the price my father must have paid in terms of promotions and raises for leaving "on time" to watch us play
sports. It wasn't until I became an adult with the similar
choices that I realized the choice my father made every day
and every week in favor of being there for us.

That was a large part of his legacy to me. When you
come to this country as an immigrant, with the life you're
used to and your possessions taken away from you, you do
what it takes to survive. You work hard, one step after
another. More importantly, he showed me that once you
become a parent, you must constantly make significant
choices in favor of those who come behind you.

Extend a Helping Hand to Those Coming Up Behind You

A man who retired after a successful career in journalism
says the best part of it all, the most gratifying and the most
fun, was "being mentored and then mentoring others." As
a young guy recently out of college, Ralph says, "I got a job
on a little paper back in Ohio, and I was so incredibly fortunate to have the most remarkable man as a boss. He took
me under his wing and spent the time needed to show me
what I was getting wrong and what I was getting right. He
was a steely-eyed man who hardly ever cracked a smile, so
you didn't love him. He had high standards regarding the

quality of the work and didn't mince his words. He wasn't about to cushion the blow when you were falling short. Yet he was able to convey these hard messages with great kindness. It wasn't personal, it wasn't about you; it was about the work.

"He set the bar for me in terms of what it took to be a mentor. At every stop on the way after that first job, I sought out someone of that ilk. And I was lucky, I suppose, to find that person every time. There's a very special quality to good mentoring, because the individual has to be both practical and business-minded and at the same time believe genuinely in the value—the rightness, you might say—of handing down acquired wisdom and bringing along a younger generation or a greener worker. It's self-serving in the best sense, because it reflects well on you and you feel good about yourself, and it's altruistic."

Ralph ended his career as a senior vice president of a major communications organization, and at his farewell parties several people spoke about how he'd helped them along. "These were mostly individuals who didn't work for me directly. They'd sought me out for various kinds of advice along the way, and those relationships in some cases stretched over years. They've all done well. And well not just in the sense of attaining good positions in good companies but in the sense of adhering to high standards of behavior. I think I had a role in that. That's enormously pleasing."

In my own career, I have also known the pleasing experience of being mentored and of mentoring others.

Many companies these days have formal mentoring programs, where an employee is assigned to someone higher up who can be a teacher and advisor. In other workplaces, ambitious and smart people hunt up their own mentors. If you are so blessed—and I believe it is a blessing—to be sought out by one or two individuals coming up the path, I'd say your heart is clearly in the right place. Take the role seriously and operate in wisdom:

- Devote time to develop a relationship. Have lunch. Be available.

- Give open and honest feedback. Show how a situation could have been better handled. Talk about what's going well and about areas that need more growth.

- Help your mentee navigate the politics and the structure of the company. Help him or her learn the environment. Point him or her toward the right people to talk to, those who are problem-solvers.

- Work out a career game plan.

- Don't assume that your advice must be followed and don't be offended if it isn't. Offer the best you have to offer, and that's the best you can do. The rest is optional.

- Sometimes, extending a helping hand
  means being a champion for an individual you perceive as worthy. You've seen the
  work he or she can do. You've seen him or
  her act with integrity and as a good steward
  of his or her job. Go to bat for her when
  maybe she can't go to bat alone. Get him
  known by the people and in the places he
  might not be able to get to alone, so that
  his work is noticed. This person might
  never realize the role you've played. Lots
  of times the champion remains an unsung
  hero. But that's part of your legacy on this
  earth.

As you move through a career, you become both mentee and mentor. You start as the one being mentored, and
then evolve into the mentoring role or the champion. But
along the way, it's important to be willing to stay the mentee as well, because it is in that relationship, where there's
open, honest dialogue and feedback, that you're going to
keep growing. It's always a mistake to believe you have
achieved a level at which you understand or know it all.
None of us ever gets there.

Share Your Story

An elementary school in my town invited me to speak to some of its students on its annual diversity day. There I was, facing a room full of thoroughly hip third graders, and wondering how to connect with them on an emotional level. I had an idea.

"Okay, here's what I want everybody to do," I said. "We're going to play a little game. I want you all to put your heads down on your desks and close your eyes."

They looked at me as if they were thinking, *You need to get a grip, lady. Give us a break!* But I was a guest and they were polite children, so they did what I asked.

"Now imagine that you're at home in your room. Picture your room. It's nighttime, you're lying in your bed, and you're almost asleep. Is everybody there? Yes? All right, now imagine there's a knock on your door, and your parents come in with some strange men. You're taken on a bus somewhere, and everything in your room you have to leave behind. All your games, your computers, books, toys—it all gets left.

"You go on a very long ride that lasts the whole night, and in the morning, you wind up in an airport. They put you on a plane, and you're going to someplace you've never been before, and you know you can never come back."

I said, "Okay, stop. Everybody open your eyes and put your heads up."

Now I had them.

I explained that the story I just told them described the beginning of my childhood. That's how I came to United States. I talked about what my life then was like, about not knowing English at first, about what my parents taught me that helped me to become a professional, and about the importance of doing well in school. They might have been still stuck on *Whoa! Leaving all my stuff behind in my room!*

I've spoken at that school several times, maybe making some small steps in broadening understanding. This has been a large part of what I see as my contribution and the legacy I can pass on. I speak in various outlets about Hispanic issues, women mentoring women, creating diversity programs. I'm often asked to talk about how I came to grow in my career, and to offer career advice to other women who want to become executives. That's a big chunk of my life story.

But each of us has a story to tell. What is yours?

Remember That You Leave a Legacy Whether You Intend to or Not

Todd, a chef, says this: "We have family dinners at home—not every night, because everybody's going in ten directions. But at least a couple of evenings a week, we all—me, my wife, the four kids—sit down and eat together and we talk about stuff.

"I've always talked about my work. You start as a prep guy, and then you're a grill guy; you move up. Two of the kids, one boy, one girl, are interested in what I do for a living. The other two, a boy and a girl, could care less. However, if I mention something about how I screwed up on the job that day, they all listen. You see it. Their little ears are flapping. Kids love nothing better than hearing how Dad screwed up. They suck it all in. So I tell those stories.

"Obviously, this isn't about big-scale disasters. I'll say how I blew my stack, really lashed out at some guy, totally lost it. Then, how I repaired the damages, or how I was going to do that the next day. I told them recently about me having to fire somebody, this kid who was just not making it. They were intrigued. Why do you get fired? If you have to fire somebody, what do you say?

"I think this is a hang-up with parents: We're always asking the kids how they're doing, pumping them for their stuff, but we don't tell how we're doing. We think we're supposed to be heroes. [We're supposed to be] role models. But not heroes. Because who's a hero in this life, really? If you don't let your kids know where you messed up and how you made it right, what do they ever learn? And I've had a couple of tough stories, times when I didn't stand up for the right thing in a small way, and I've talked about those times, too. I think this is what you leave your kids, a way to handle what's going on in your life. You talk about the times you mess up and how you try to fix it."

You don't always realize that everyone around you is learning from what you are doing and going through. It's not just about you. Everyone is watching. The audience is listening. So as you go through life, the people near to you are getting something from your actions. It may not even be acknowledged in the time span you may want, but it's happening.

Here is how to
CREATE A LEGACY:

- Reach out to those who are not like you.

- Be there for children.

- Extend a helping hand to those coming up behind you.

- Share your story.

- Remember that you leave a legacy whether you intend to or not.

PART THREE

On Reflection

EIGHT

Things I Used to Believe That I No Longer Believe Today

I AM NOT THE SAME PERSON that I was three years ago. Three years from now, I will not be exactly the same as I am today. Growth and change are part of life. A journey of a lifetime implies movement. For me, for each of us, movement inevitably means that there are people we will leave behind, thoughts we will no longer think, and beliefs we will no longer hold dear. If you keep churning on with the identical thoughts, habits, and plans, doing the same old things in the same old ways year after year, you don't get far.

In the course of writing this book, I've been on a different kind of journey, a mental one of recollections. Thinking back over the experiences I describe in these chapters, from my childhood as an immigrant girl in Miami and through twenty years of a wide-ranging career, I've been interested in sorting out what was then and what is now. What ideas have I abandoned, as work experiences and my deepening relationship with God altered my sights? What others have held true?

I want to share some of those conclusions with you. They are inextricably bound with the challenge of leading a Spirit-led career and striving always to live up to the spiritual principles it requires: faith, prayerfulness, humility, integrity, forgiveness, stewardship, and creating a legacy.

Maybe some of my insights will echo ones you have discovered for yourself as you have followed your own career path.

FORMER BELIEF 1:

A Woman Needs to Act as Tough as a Man to Succeed in a Work Environment

We tend to hold certain stereotypical ideas about how men are supposed to act on the job and how women are supposed to act. Women are the nurturing, collaborative ones; men are the independent, aggressive ones. Not necessarily.

I was always aware, at the beginning, that the business world was largely a man's world or a boy's club, and I knew that an ambitious woman had better learn to navigate that foreign territory. But some of the things I learned from my parents were to remain gracious and not to let others dictate my limitations. "Don't listen to fear and ignorance," they said. Don't let anyone tell you there's something in business you cannot achieve because you are a woman."

But probably because all my earliest experiences of corporate life occurred in exclusively male groups, there were lessons to learn about adapting to a prevailing atmosphere. And yet I realized that there is power and strength in being a woman in the workplace. We bring with us a unique set of skills and talents different from those men bring. When we try to be anything other than who we are, we leave a void that cannot be replaced.

FORMER BELIEF 2:

Women Naturally Will Help Other Women

Theoretically, it sounds right that women naturally help other women. In practice, it doesn't always work out that way.

Women don't always help each other out just because they're women. I've worked with some wonderful women and some wonderful men, and it's a mistake to assume a common bond because of a shared gender. When I talk to young women just starting on careers, I always stress the wisdom of searching out role models and mentoring opportunities where you can get them. Look for empathetic and generous people with a wide range of expertise, not just those most like you.

As I mentioned in a previous chapter, early in my career I had a female boss. My inclination was to be completely forthright with her. I believed instinctively in a natural camaraderie between us. We were both women; we shared similar goals, challenges, and struggles. Over time, however, I came to realize that she found some of my job initiatives potentially threatening to her position and was working behind the scenes to eliminate my job.

On the other hand, I have throughout my career enjoyed and benefited from extremely positive mentoring relationships with men. Being at more advanced career stages, having broader and longer experience, these individuals were able to teach me what I needed to know to get to the next level.

FORMER BELIEF 3:
You Succeed in the Workplace Only by Giving Up or Putting on Hold Personal Achievements or Desires

I used to believe this wholeheartedly for a long time. Those were my workaholic days: I was single, spending insane hours at my job and traveling most of the month, and then I'd go to church. Not much else was happening.

But one of the lessons I learned over those years—and it took being laid up with pneumonia and a few other trials to get it—was that life should not slide out of balance because you are single or on your own. Not having the priorities of spouse or of your own family doesn't justify absorbing all your attention and filling all your hours with work. That's a life out of whack. Career successes may come, but that isn't the same as living out God's full purpose for your time on this earth. We are called to be worthy stewards of our lives, not just of our jobs.

I came to understand that there was a purpose for the single stage in my life. But the purpose wasn't for me to work longer than the married people, to put everything else on hold since there wasn't much else happening anyway. That's an easy habit to slip into, because both your inclinations and outside pressures promote it. In some work environments, there used to be, if not still is, a general assumption on the job that the unattached woman or man will pick up any slack, cover the bases. He or she doesn't have family to get home to, after all.

These are tough issues. Studies have indicated that single workers, especially women, feel taken advantage of and overloaded, because the mother must leave early for a soccer game or come to work late because of a parent–teacher meeting or stay home with a sick child. And while single men may have certain career opportunities, when layoffs or reorganizations come, there's pressure to keep those employees who are their family's main providers.

Over time, and it did take time, I began to establish better boundaries. I let it be known that I was not available for fifteen-hour days, every day.

Being single can include lonely moments. It can also be a truly unique time for building and enhancing the foundation of a relationship with God—specifically because you don't have the priorities of marriage and family pulling at you. You come to know yourself. You grow to realize that your calling is just as important in the kingdom of God as is the calling of one who's married and raising children. You learn to value yourself. When you understand how important you are to God, it does something for your self-worth and your self-esteem. You're no longer defined by job titles and labels, by married or unmarried. And that, in turn, enables you to stand a lot more firmly when you're setting boundaries in the workplace.

Many single people say, in effect, *I can worry about the God thing later; when my career is well under way, then I'll do something about my spiritual life.* Tomorrow is not promised to any of us, however. We don't know what the next day holds. I discovered over time that if you make God, that primary relationship, your foundation for how you live and make decisions regarding your career, you will make even better decisions in choosing a partner when that becomes your new calling. Every stage of life has its blessings, if we elect to connect with God in a way that allows Him to show us what those are.

There's a verse of scripture that says: "Taste and see that the Lord is good." In other words, experience it for yourself. Though sometimes the path is obscured, sometimes has fiery trials, and sometimes seems dark to you, when you look back, you say, *Wow, thank you. That time strengthened me.*

Can you have it all, as the saying goes? I say yes, absolutely. I am proof, if only to myself, that an ongoing career and a fully rounded personal life are not incompatible. Of course, reality and common sense should tell us that having it all will probably come over time, perhaps even over a lifetime, probably not all arriving as one grand present simultaneously.

FORMER BELIEF 4:

Doing the Right Thing Is Enough to Get You Where You Want to Go

The principles I've described throughout this book are all really about doing the right thing. That is, act with humility and integrity and with forgiveness and compassion. Be a good steward of the people and the companies you work with, and help those coming up behind. But I hope I have also conveyed the message that right actions go hand in hand with a strong sense of self-worth.

Know your value. Be informed about the worth of your skills in the workplace and ask for what you deserve based on performance. Strategize your career moves and be assertive about hunting up the people and opportunities that will get you onto the next step. And if, like some of the individuals who have shared their stories here, you're thinking of striking out in bold, scary new directions, try to have your financial and other ducks in a row.

I've written about times I negotiated my salaries, argued for new positions, and so on. I may have sounded fearless. I wasn't always, and it took some years to learn to be bold. We'd all probably prefer to do the right thing, be good, produce on the job, and then sit back and wait for the world to notice and come up with appropriate rewards. But the world doesn't always work that way. Sometimes, you must speak up.

It's easier to feel self-confident when it comes from purpose being driven by God. Developing God confidence enables you to be bold when it's time to be bold.

You Need to Have All the Answers

One of my wise bosses taught me a crucial lesson. People will respect you as much for your willingness to find out what you don't know, he said, as for what you do know. As a workaholic and overachiever, that was a message I truly had to embrace. You do not always need all the answers; you do need to reach out to individuals from a variety of areas and backgrounds, pull people together in team approaches, and leverage their expertise and insight.

It is a strength, much more than a weakness, to acknowledge what you don't know and to learn from others. We can tend to be too hard on ourselves—focus on our deficiencies and where we need improvement, and think we must struggle through on our own. Reaching out to others is the better way.

FORMER BELIEF 6:

You Have a Work Persona and a Nonwork Persona

Not so. You are who you are all the time. If you're a self-serving person, you're not empathetic, you don't listen well, and let's say you lose your temper in a hurry—that's always right there with you. The quality may come out glaringly with one individual and not with another, but it's still present.

Here's where home life ties in with professional life. You can't "check it at the door," turning off part of yourself in the office and picking it up again when you get home.

Not really. It's not human nature to divide yourself that way. It's not Ana the professional who is impatient. It's Ana the human being who is impatient. If I learn to look at my shortcomings in one area, then I can see them in other places and with other people in my life, and I can work to improve.

That often starts with the prayer *Oh, God, save me from myself.*

NINE

Things I Used to Believe That I Believe More Strongly Today

ℛROUND THE TIME I first formed a relationship with God in the way I described earlier, I set down for myself a goal, my personal mission statement: to live a life worthy of the calling I have within me and be worthy of the sacrifices my parents made, in order that I might take advantage of unique opportunities. I believe everyone should have a personal mission statement for their life.

On reflection, I'm examining how I've lived up to that goal so far and the sustaining beliefs that held true through the years. Here are the big ones.

BELIEF 1:

Never Forget Where You Came From and How You Started

An interviewer once asked me whom I would most like to meet. I thought about individuals I've come in contact with in my career—several presidents, ambassadors, movie stars, celebrities, interesting and influential people. And I said I would most like to meet my three grandparents who died before I got to know them. I believe they could give me a much richer understanding of my history and perspective on my family. I would love to know how they helped to shape the characters of my mother and father, who ultimately shaped me. I would also like to know what they were like as kids.

The grandmother I did know lived with us in Miami until she died, when I was twelve. Her death affected me deeply. She and I spent many hours together, and I knew her probably better than my siblings did. My grandfather's business had moved them to Cuba from Spain decades earlier, and she initially resisted joining us on our flight to Florida, announcing that she did not intend to uproot herself again. But my parents insisted, and so she was a strong and stable presence in my life. From her and from my mother, we kids learned about Cuban authors, the poets, and Spanish writers such as Cervantes. They both always tuned in to the political shows and commentary on the radio, watching Walter Cronkite on TV, investing time in the news, "something real, something substantial," my mom said.

I think of those two women, not fluent in the language, always looking forward, always learning. I think of their courage.

Look forward. That was the message. Interestingly, my parents never wanted us, as young adults, to return to Cuba, not even for a visit. They did not want us to see what the country had become. Their feeling was "It's not our country anymore; it's not how we want you to remember it." But there was always a desire in my heart to see that place, and I finally had a chance on a mission trip with my church. I was able to meet uncles and other relatives, spend a day with them, these people I had not known and who hadn't seen me since I was two. I had a taste of all the forces that had come together to start us on a new life, and what had been ingrained in my parents because of that time and place.

They always told us: "Governments can take things from you, whatever they want, but they cannot take who you are; they cannot take the knowledge and the breeding you possess." My mom and dad put a lot of stock in those values. So a big focus for us always was school—studying, doing well in classes, thinking what career all that might lead to. They never talked about the need for us to marry and give them grandchildren, for example; they believed

God would take care of that at the right moment. Getting a proper education, establishing a successful career will not take care of itself in many ways; achieving those goals requires conscious thought and effort, and a lot of prayer.

That's where I came from and how I started. That's something I never want to forget.

BELIEF 2:

Honor Your Father and Your Mother

Honor your father and your mother, regardless of who they are, what they did, where they come from, what they don't know. Chances are, they know a whole lot more than you might think.

My parents have been among my biggest supporters in my career, the ones I always go to for advice. There were times along the way when I called them repeatedly to get their perspective. Not because they were going to help me with the present value of the dollar or draw up the latest, greatest communication strategy I needed for my job. But I could always ask, "What do you think about this?" Often, their suggestions about handling the people-related issues I faced were far wiser than some of the advice I'd hear from individuals who were maybe more "successful" or knowledgeable.

Your parents don't have to be Rhodes Scholars to understand the dynamics of human nature. They have insights you don't have. I come from a culture where you respect your elders, because gray hair means experience.

I've thought about that notion of honoring one's parents and what it means. To honor your parents can take on many forms. In a basic way it means that you give them your time, that they are a priority for you. It also means putting them first where appropriate. It means sharing your life with them, the success and the failures. It means not judging their actions; we will never walk in their shoes. It means forgiving them for the times they made mistakes.

Part of honoring them also is following what they have taught you, as long as it is not unethical, immoral, or ungodly. For me, it goes back to those earliest days when I was starting out on my journey when God gave me the courage to say to my parents, "I won't flounder spiritually. I have to follow what's in my heart. Thank you for giving me a strong foundation, but I'm being led in another direction." You see, my parents had taught me to find my own way in life and to follow opportunities as they arose, and I was living up to that.

My dad was a great balance to what was going on during that time. His words were "Don't worry how I'm going to react. You do what you need to do, what you feel is right. As long as it's not illegal or immoral or goes against God, the rest will work out."

I've always been proud of my parents. Until just a year

ago, I'd return home every six weeks for a long weekend, just to hang out with them. We definitely travel in different worlds. I remember one time I'd been invited to a cocktail party at the White House. I'd forgotten to tell my folks, so I called them from the airport on my way to Washington, D.C.: "Hey, guys, you'll never guess where I'm going tonight." On the other side of the phone, my mom and dad, on different extensions, were speechless. It dawned on me the impact my news was having on them.

Two weeks later I flew home for one of those long weekends. I was lying on the couch reading. I had on jeans with holes in the knees and an old T-shirt. My mom came over and said, "I don't know if I've told you lately how proud of you your father and I are. You surpassed anything we could have done years ago. But you know what we like the most? How down to earth you're still remaining. People tell me you talk about us so well, you always bring us up, and you've never been ashamed of us." The look on my mother's face and the mist in her eyes spoke more than even those words that meant the world to me.

BELIEF 3:

Find a Career Path That Brings Out Your Passion and Sense of Urgency

You may be a great leader, a terrific boss, but you cannot teach a single one of your employees to have passion.

It is, in a very real way, part of the raw material we come into the world with.

When you discover your career path, the one that taps into your unique wiring, that in and of itself will unlock passion. It may not happen immediately, but as you step forward and see events unfolding and experience growth, the passion will kick in. When I started my career, I had no idea the road would lead me to some of the places I have gone. But with each step, I recognized more of how the puzzle was coming together and how much my innate talents actually fit in an arena I had never even considered.

But I would caution that passion is not excitement or even enthusiasm. It's deeper, something you feel even when the situation of the moment isn't going so well. Your passion is for what you do and the impact it has; it isn't based on immediate circumstances around you. I absolutely love what I do and have often carried it out in work environments that were far from great at times.

We tend to think that doctors or ministers or teachers, perhaps, will feel passionate about their work and their careers. They have "a calling." We tend not to make the passion connection with people in business arenas. I believe you do not have to be involved in an altruistic endeavor to be passionate. What you do will dictate your passion. The minister, the teacher, and the Wall Street executive, too—each has been uniquely formed by God to accomplish his or her calling, in those ways. And a minister, a teacher, or a Wall Street executive can also miss the mark of that calling.

I sometimes equate this issue of passion or the passionate calling with the idea of urgency. In the most basic sense, that means getting the job done. Not dragging your feet. As a manager, I have at times seen people dillydallying on a project or assignment, and often it's because they believe there will be opposition to what they're asked to accomplish. Or they are not sure how to go about doing things, and they're reluctant or unable to ask for direction. I've also worked with people who have mentally and spiritually checked out of the job. These persons are no longer fully engaged, not passionate about seeing results. That's a loss for everyone.

Some people start out with high hopes, finding what they're doing promising or enjoyable. Then the years go by, and one day they think, *Is this all there is?* or *Is this the kind of work I should have pursued?* or *I'm only at this now because I've built up experience here and I need the income and there aren't a lot of other jobs around, so what now?*

There are no easy answers. So many real-life factors influence us. Clearly, if you're supporting a family, you need the paycheck and you need the benefits. If there are limited opportunities in your field, then maintaining a feeling of passion for your work might come low on the list of your priorities. However, I do think that reaching a point of worry or disappointment or "Is this all there is?" can be a critical one in terms of your one and only, unique life. My response probably will not surprise you: Have faith in God's purpose. Let faith rather than fear or frustration guide you. When in doubt—pray.

BELIEF 4:

Challenges Can Either Break You and Stunt Your Growth or Cause You to Rise Up and Achieve Your Best

Which way you go when faced with a challenge—let it break you or let it motivate you to achieve your best—is a personal choice.

Take on a challenge as a positive opportunity—take it on with integrity, humility, and courage—and I believe that in the midst of all the stuff, you will discover what I have: that you will come across folks who get it and who will take you under their wing. You will find that some organizations want to do the right thing but don't know how; that there are advantages to be gained by stepping onto new ground, even though those steps are difficult or even painful; that being in the ranks of trailblazers, you can shape the course of your career and the lives of those around you.

God Never Acts in Random Ways

Being single was a great time in my life. Being married is great, too.

There is a passage of scripture that speaks to my husband and me, probably because we're both professionals: "Two are better than one, because they have a good reward for their labor; for if they fall, one will lift his companion up.... Though one may be overpowered by another, two can withstand him. And a threefold cord is not easily broken."

That cord is you, your partner, and God, who binds you together.

But because two is better than one doesn't mean that being one isn't the best, during the periods you are called to be one. And sometimes these periods might be puzzling.

My husband and I were able to look back over our first year of marriage and see how God permitted events to come into our lives that forced two very independent older people to depend on each other. Returning from the honeymoon, I was immediately bedridden with a bout of walking pneumonia, and my husband took care of me. A little further down the line, he had serious back surgery, and I took care of him. Then we learned that I was pregnant. A lot was going on during our first year of marriage.

Some friends said, "Boy, you guys have had bad luck,

bad timing." I don't think so. First of all, we don't believe in luck. Luck means random events, outside of God's control. We don't believe there's anything outside God's control. We look at what happened and see the hand of God in it. We see how He's allowed certain events, and those have brought us closer together and caused us to stretch new muscles: *How do I depend on another person? How do I come to the place where I become one with another person? How do I trust someone totally?* When you're flat on your back and you can't do for yourself, you come to the realization *I need this other person.* And there's nothing stronger. If being flattened is what it takes, then bring it on.

Again, it's born out of having a sense of purpose; it's understanding that in the end, God works all that happens in our lives for the good of those who love Him, not for bad. In your personal life, in your work life, there's a reason for what's happening. Be still and let Him show you the reason.

BELIEF 6:

You Reap What You Sow, Always

The lesson that you always reap what you sow was one I saw unfold with one of my earlier bosses whom I mentioned in a previous chapter. She thought I wanted her job, and she tried to have mine eliminated during an organizational restructuring. I went on to a bigger, better position, and she wound up being restructured out of the organization. I have seen this play out a dozen times over. It does not always happen immediately or in the same way or between the same two people, but we all reap what we sow sooner or later.

This goes for the good as well as bad. Good seeds sown bear good fruit. The people we mentor, the integrity we live with, and all of the principles covered in this book, they all come back to visit us, and our children and those who come after us as well will reap good fruit from the good seeds we have sown.

Afterword

I began *Keeping the Faith* with the words of seventeenth-century mathematician, philosopher, and inventor Blaise Pascal: "There is a God-shaped vacuum in the heart of every man which cannot be filled by any created thing, but only by God the Creator, made known through Jesus Christ."

In spite of his towering intellect, this man of mathematics and science believed that without God, life has no meaning. You were made for God, not vice versa, Pascal was saying. Life is about letting Him use you for His purpose, not using Him for your own purpose. I believe that each one of us is at some level profoundly aware of that God-shaped vacuum in our heart. A vacuum demands to be filled, and we go about it in so many ways, attempting to find our own answers or role models to follow. Sooner or later, consciously or unconsciously, we come to realize that peace, connection, and purpose can be found only with God.

Once you begin this journey with God, you are in for

the adventure of your life. Your wildest dreams will pale in comparison with what God has in store for you. I often think back to my dreams as an eighteen-year-old, my hopes and ambitions. And then I surrendered my life to God, and I can honestly say that by the time I was in my late twenties, my life had exceeded those wildest dreams and expectations.

Perhaps especially today, the events and people shaping the headlines have paved the way for resurgence in the belief that our spiritual lives must be more alive, more deeply imbedded in everyday decisions and actions. The answers to your life, finding your own purpose in the world, come from asking the Creator—and from establishing that relationship that penetrates the details of all of life. This is paramount.

Throughout *Keeping the Faith*, I've often used the word *purpose*. When I talk about purpose, I have in mind three levels of meaning. There's the overarching meaning: I am placed here for a reason, something to accomplish that will cover the expanse of my life, so that I will look back one day and recognize a fulfilled role.

Then there's the sense of purpose that involves times of change or redirection, the roads or even seeming detours that appear along the way and that I know I am meant to follow. I have faith that just as it happens in the weaving of a tapestry, the final canvas will make sense and form a whole; each thread exists because it must.

Finally, I think of everyday purpose, the many, many steps and decisions as I go through the routines of my day—working with others, getting my immediate jobs done, dealing in a godly way with difficulties or frustrations.

Much of this book has been about everyday purpose as it relates to work. A popular expression tells us that "the devil is in the details." I believe that God is in the details. All of the spiritual principles I've outlined here sum up a lifestyle or work style, one that's reflective or representative of a relationship with God. That lifestyle plays out or is revealed in the details of our life:

- Seek out the wisdom and support of others who have greater knowledge and experience than you. Then reach out to those who could benefit from your knowledge and experience and help them along.

- Be a responsible steward of the responsibilities and the tasks you've been given to accomplish your job.

- Have tough conversations when you know they're necessary, even though they're difficult and uncomfortable.

- Place appropriate value on your skills and talents.

- Act with integrity, even if nobody else knows or does.

- Offer an apology when you have unintentionally belittled or hurt another.

- Refuse to condone or take part in wrong actions.

- Remember that sometimes it's what you don't say, not what you say.

- Above all else, surrender and pray for God's unique purpose for you.

In living out a career with God as the center, the details count. When you have established that relationship with God, the attitudes of your heart and mind lead to godly actions—and people notice.

My three perspectives on purpose all connect, one to the other. Above all is the sense of God's mission and calling, and the journey. Without having Him, I cannot be disciplined and focused about what I need to do to get there, because I don't have a "there" to get to. Without Him, humility, integrity, forgiveness, all the principles I believe in, don't hold much relevance. They become abstractions, easy to give lip service to but easy also to ignore, forget, or override when the going gets tough.

Acknowledgments

"I thank my God upon every remembrance of you."

PHILIPPIANS 1:3

WORDS CANNOT ADEQUATELY EXPRESS the amount of thanksgiving I have in my heart for the many people—friends, family, and colleagues—who helped make this book a reality through their prayers and support.

With loving gratitude to my husband, John: Thank you for believing that I could do this when I didn't, for your desire that I be all that the Lord has created me to be, for your love and support during this process, and for your prayers. I love you always.

To my daughter, Sydney Isabel: May you grow to be all that God has destined you to be, giving thanks to Him always.

To my stepson, Justin: Your spirit and focus on God's will for your life is an example to all around you; you are a blessing to us all.

Where would I be if not for my parents, Pablo and Ana Mollinedo? They taught me the foundation of everything I share in this book, but most importantly, they taught me to seek God always and in all things. Your love and sacrifice have meant the world to me. Thanks, Mom and Dad.

To my sister, Marlene, and my brother, Peter: Your unconditional excitement over my successes has always overwhelmed me. Thank you for being in my corner and believing in me even when you didn't always understand. You have both served as inspirations in this project in more ways than you know.

For my dear friends who spoke words of wisdom and encouragement at every turn of this process—Jennifer Marr, Marilyn Sims, Sylvia Benito, Isabel Rivera, Kathryn Min, Akram and David Tobias, Elizabeth Lisboa-Farrow, Anna Escobedo Cabral, Betty Cortina, Sabrina Womack, Tony, Darlene, and Kristen Rogers: Each of you has influenced this process in a special and unique way. To Haydee Morales, for planting a seed that continues to bear fruit. Thanks to Pastor Neil and Noline Rhodes for your unconditional love and spiritual guidance that has always caused me to press forward in Christ.

Many thanks to Isabel Gonzalez, friend, author, editor,

for believing in me more than I believed in myself and igniting the spark that started all this.

To my agent, Harvey Klinger, for guiding me through the ins and outs of the publishing world: Thank you for your wisdom, your humor, and your chutzpah. You understood me from the beginning, and for that I am truly grateful. To Andrea Thompson: Thank you for capturing my thoughts and giving them life. You are awesome! Thanks to my very talented publisher, Rene Alegria, who believed in me and this book from the beginning; to my associate publisher, Raymond Garcia; and to the wonderful Harper/Rayo team: Melinda Moore, Amy Vreeland, Larry Hughes, and countless others.

As well, I give a debt of gratitude to the many people who willingly shared their time and life stories for this book. While their names and identifying details have been changed here in order to protect their privacy, their experiences added to the scope and depth that make *Keeping the Faith* come alive. Thank you!

To my God and Lord, Christ Jesus: Everything I am and everything I have I owe to you. Thank you for the privilege.